Women Invent

Two Centuries of Discoveries That Have Shaped Our World

SUSAN
CASEY

CHICAGO
REVIEW
PRESS

Library of Congress Cataloging-in-Publication Data

Casey, Susan (Susan Mary)
        Women invent: two centuries of discoveries that have shaped our world /
by Susan Casey.
                        p.   cm.
        Includes bibliographical references and index.
        Summary: Uses short biographies of women inventors around the world
to demonstrate how inventions come about.
        ISBN 978-1-55652-317-5 (paper)
        1. Women inventors — Biography — Juvenile literature. 2. Inventions —
History — Juvenile literature. 3. Children as inventors — Juvenile literature. [1.
Inventions — History. 2. Inventors. 3. Women — Biography.] I. Title.
T39.C38 1997
604'82-dc21   97-18870
                                                                  CIP
                                                                  AC

© 1997 by Susan Casey
All rights reserved
First edition
Published by Chicago Review Press, Incorporated
814 North Franklin Street
Chicago, Illinois 60610
ISBN 978-1-55652-317-5
Printed in the United States of America
10 9 8 7 6 5

To my mother, Joan Hampton Casey

Contents

Acknowledgments

I WOULD LIKE to thank Carolyn See and Dr. Joseph Lifschutz who were both significant in my development as a writer. In the course of writing this book, I received invaluable help and assistance from many people and extend a sincere thank you to all of them. In particular, I want to thank Helen Haskell and Billie Connor of the Los Angeles Public Library Patent Department, Ruth Nyblod of the U.S. Patent and Trademark Office, and patent lawyer Charles Schroeder. I greatly benefitted from the suggestions of several classroom teachers who make invention an integral part of their curriculum: Sue Windham, Nancy Gerardy, Pat Bradel, and Nick Frankovits. Douglas Scharmann, Rachelle Romberg, and Lillian Ross provided extensive and invaluable suggestions. I am also grateful to my young readers, Nicole Hutchinson and Zane Welte, and to their mothers, Pamela Hutchinson and Patsy Casey, for encouraging them to help me.

Thanks also to my friends. Rachel Clark's weekly encouragement helped tremendously. The support of Mary Rose and Stephen O'Leary; Susan Brooke; Scotty Embree; Donvieve, Richie, Bob, and Deanna Drake; and Louise and Bernice Sheehy sustained me. And many thanks go to Jimmy and Alma Casey who fed me when I staggered in from the library; to Bill Welte, Mike and Tina Casey, Kevin and Bobbie Casey, and Katie Casey and Russ Anderson for their interest; and to Brian, Jason, Eric, Carlos, Mikie, Nathan, Karissa, and Micah Casey; Carson Welte; and Christine Anderson for being their wonderful selves.

Sincere thanks to my editor, Cynthia Sherry, for her helpful comments and open-mindedness and for her sunny disposition.

Last, but most important, I would like to thank all the inventors, their families, and the companies affiliated with their inventions for their generous cooperation and support.

2

Introduction

When I was a girl, the comic book character I most enjoyed was the inventor Gyro Gearloose. He was so enthusiastic about having ideas, and each time he got a new one, a lightbulb would appear. That was the way I, too, felt when I got an idea. I liked that feeling. I still do.

As I grew older, my fascination with inventors and inventing continued. When my friend Laurel Gaiser's father, Conrad, invented Bounce, the antistatic tissue, I was thrilled to know an actual inventor. My interest in his thought process led me to wonder about the stories behind the invention of other household items and eventually to write a magazine article about women inventors.

As part of my research I spoke with many inventors. Each told an engrossing story about the discovery of her invention. As soon as I finished hearing one tale, I wanted to hear another. Then I began reading about the lives of eighteenth- and nineteenth-century inventors. Since I couldn't talk with them, I read their patents.

While many history books depict women as "just being around," and many books on inventors give little evidence of women's work, the patent records reveal a different story. In her 1917 patent, May

Conner of Garden Grove, Iowa, describes her hay-handling device, an intricate system of ropes and pulleys connected with a hayfork and a carriage. To write of it May could not have been merely "around her farm"; she had to have been in the barn measuring distances and angles, figuring weights, and plotting directions. She was a busy, thinking woman. And I discovered every other woman inventor to be the same. I grew to admire each one. I hope that my depiction of their involvements and their activities does justice to their remarkable accomplishments. I am honored to tell their stories.

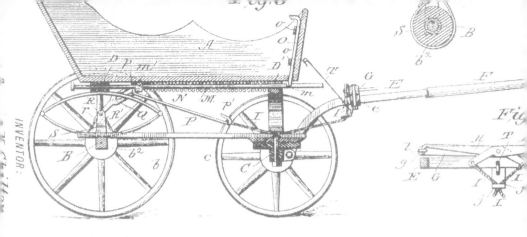

1 *Necessity Calls*

"We still live in a world in which a significant fraction of people, including women, believe that a woman belongs —and wants to belong —exclusively in the home. . . . The world cannot afford the loss of the talents of half of its people if we are to solve the many problems which beset us."
— Dr. Rosalyn Yalow, Nobel Prize winner, 1977

The horse trotted at a steady pace, pulling the open carriage. It was a pleasant day in the mid-1880s in Baltimore, Maryland. The family riding in the countryside, especially the mother and father, talked of the birds that flitted about. Their daughter was too busy to chat. She was watching the birds as they flew from branch to branch. Then a loud blast, an explosion, frightened the horse. The little girl turned to look and saw the horse rear — saw its front hooves fly into the air and then down again. The carriage rocked unsteadily. Her mother and father held onto her and the carriage. Then the horse began to run, gallop, too fast, much too fast. The carriage was tipping to one side, then another. The little girl screamed. How were they going to get the carriage free of the runaway horse?

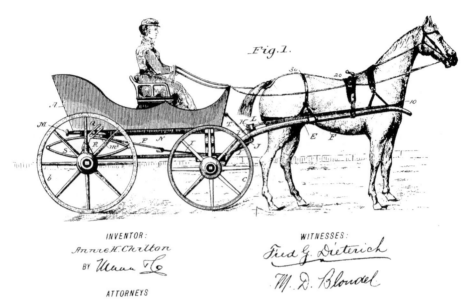

Fig.1.

INVENTOR:

Annie H. Chilton

BY *Munn & Co*

ATTORNEYS

WITNESSES:

Fred G. Dieterich

M. D. Blondel

Patent drawing for Annie Chilton's Horse Detacher and Brake.

That was exactly the question Annie Chilton answered when she invented a device that would do just that. In 1891, the Baltimore woman gained a patent for a Horse Detacher and Brake, a device that would prevent accidents like the one about to happen in the story above.

Annie saw a problem that needed to be solved. Then she created a solution with her invention. She is only one of many women inventors, before and after her, who did the same.

So what are inventions, exactly? An invention is a discovery of something new that is useful to people. People might see it and say, "Wow, that's great. I could use that." Like what?

In 1976, in another part of the world, Magdalena (Maggie) Villaruz of the Philippines wanted to grow rice in the fields of her farm, but the fields were very wet. Tractors used to cultivate the wet fields got stuck in the mud. That is, until Maggie invented Turtle

Power Tillers, a small tractor that can be pushed by hand. It doesn't get stuck in the mud; it floats. She obtained a patent in the United Kingdom and Japan in 1981. She has since gained nineteen other patents for inventions of farming machinery and was awarded the International Federation of Inventors' Association Cup as the Most Outstanding Woman Inventor of her country in 1995.

Annie needed a way to stop a runaway horse. Maggie needed to be able to farm in her fields. More than five million inventions have been patented in America, and millions of others have been patented in Canada, Europe, and other areas of the world in the last few hundred years. Inventions by women are included in those millions. Women, like men, have invented what they needed.

Women of the 1800s and early 1900s who lived on farms in America needed harvesting equipment, supplies and equipment for raising livestock and poultry, and tools for planting and tilling. So they invented and patented. Other women received patents for garden tools and equipment. Others invented insecticides to get rid of critters that killed the plants.

Anna Corey Baldwin, the wife of a dairy farmer in New Jersey, received four dairy-related patents in the 1860s and 1870s, including one for cooling milk quickly and one for gloves that promised to help speed up the milking of the cows. In 1887 Hannah Harger of Manchester, Iowa, worried about all the flies that were bothering her babies, invented and gained a patent for the screen door. In 1892, Sarah Boone, an African American woman of New Haven, Connecticut, designed an ironing board that made it easier to iron the sleeves of ladies' garments and mens' coats. In 1917 May Conner of Garden Grove, Iowa, invented a hay-handling device that used a well-planned system of ropes and pulleys to make it possible to easily transport hay to a storage area. "The object of my invention," she wrote in her patent, "is for use in stacking hay or moving hay away in a barn . . . for carrying hay along a stock or barn." Her device was connected to a carriage and to forks used to move the hay.

Decades later, in the 1990s, a much younger woman who lived on a farm thought that the world needed biodegradable containers for fast food. So Disa Rubenbauer, who was in elementary school in Marshalltown, Iowa, created a container for hamburgers and other fast food out of corn products. Because it was winter, the fields on her family's farm were full of corn stalks. Disa and her father gathered some. After Disa ground them up in a blender, she combined the mushy corn stalks with corn syrup, corn oil, corn meal, corn starch, and water. She experimented with the amounts of each ingredient and with how much time the mixture had to be baked. When she finished she had created a container that would hold food and not harm the environment. She received an award from Invent Iowa!, an invention program of Iowa schools.

Years earlier, Amanda Jones was concerned with food, too. She thought there ought to be more ways to preserve it. When Amanda, who was born in 1835, was growing up in upstate New York, she loved the outdoors. And she loved to read. Her parents thought books were important and encouraged her, and her many brothers and sisters, to read. By age fifteen Amanda was a teacher at Buffalo High School. Then her favorite brother died a sudden death. It affected her deeply and led her to an interest in spiritualism, a popular movement of the day. She conducted séances in an attempt to communicate with him and claimed to have a spiritual guide. The guide was the one who prompted her career as an inventor. He suggested that there was a way to can fruit. He left it up to Amanda to figure out the method. In 1872 she came up with the vacuum process of preserving food with the aid of her cousin, Professor Leroy C. Cooley of Albany, New York. Food was placed in a container, the air was drained out, and hot liquid was added to seal it so that it could be stored for future use. Amanda started the Woman's Canning and Preserving Company in 1890 to manufacture and sell her canned food. She had plants in several states and advertised her products in national magazines.

Amanda's inventive talents went in another direction as well. In 1880, when she was forty-five, she wanted to find a way that crude oil could be burned safely so that oil could be used as a fuel. So she visited the oil fields where drillers were extracting the oil and devised and gained Patent Number 225,839 for an Automatic Safety Burner. The U.S. Navy praised it. Amanda also pursued a career as a poet, a writer, and a magazine editor. Several books of her poems were published including *Poems* and *Ulah and Other Poems*. The poems reveal her knowledge of wildflowers and bird songs. She was also the author of five other books, including *A Psychic Autobiography*.

WOMEN WHO LIVED in cities created inventions that served the needs of city life. They gained patents for fire escapes, heaters, and floor warmers. In 1868 Mary Evard gained a patent for a stove and a broiling apparatus. She wrote in her patent application: "The meal is supported . . . upon spits suspended in a reflector before the fire. . . ." In 1895, Claytonia J. Dorticus of Newton, New Jersey, an African American, gained patents relating to her work as a photographer. One was for an invention of a photographic print washer. Another was for a machine for embossing photographs. In the early 1900s women invented different types of bicycles and motorcycles. They invented horse-drawn vehicles, traffic signals, and equipment for boats and aircraft. In 1871 Augusta Rodgers was granted Patent Number 114,605 for a device relating to railroad locomotives. The device carried smoke and cinders to the roadbed below the train rather than into the air. Another woman gained a patent for improvements in locomotive wheels. When the first automobiles appeared on roads, women invented accessories, tires, and tire attachments.

Hannah Mountain was concerned with water accidents. What do people do if they fall off a boat? So in 1873 she created and gained a patent for a life preserver—one large enough for a person to lie on.

It was approved as an auxiliary lifesaving appliance by the U.S. Supervising Inspectors of Steamboats. In 1963 *Newsweek* called Dr. Chien-Shiung Wu the "Queen of Physics," but she was also an inventor, according to *Mothers and Daughters of Invention* by Autumn Stanley. She gained patents in the field of radiation and encouraged many young women to become physicists. In the 1970s chemist Marguerite Shue-Wen Chang worked in the United States for the Department of the Navy and gained several patents related to atomic energy.

What about things for the house? Sure. Women invented heaters, trash receptacles, garment containers, insect and rodent catchers, and embroidery machines. They invented telephone and telegraphic equipment and devices for mailing packages. They invented umbrellas, trunks, and footwear.

Helen Blanchard was mechanically inclined and from a wealthy family, but when her father, a prominent shipbuilder in Maine, died and the business failed, she had to sell the family home and make a living. So she fidgeted with her sewing machine and began to think of ways to improve on it. She received her first patent in 1873 and later gained more than twenty others. She founded a company to market her inventions, made quite a profit, and bought back the family homestead.

More than a hundred years later, in the 1990s, another tinkering woman, Stella Quesnelle, from Penetanguishene, Ontario, Canada, was concerned with the effort it takes to rake all the leaves each fall. So she invented the Lawn Star Rake, a tool with wheels that makes raking faster and easier.

$$\geqslant \!\!\! \stackrel{\displaystyle \Omega}{} \!\!\! \leqslant$$

WOMEN'S IDEAS FOR inventions were for every aspect of life, yet many people of the late 1860s, the post-Civil War era, felt that the fields of architecture and construction were not suited to women. Many thought it was not proper for women to climb up on ladders or to visit construction sites as people did who worked in the those fields. Harriet Irwin of North Carolina disagreed. She was the daughter of Robert Hall Morrison, the president of Davidson College in North Carolina, who taught her that women could do many different jobs. That's why he sent Harriet to college. After finishing college, Harriet, at age twenty, married James Irwin. As they

Harriet Irwin's six-sided house. Courtesy of the Public Library of Charlotte-Meckleburg County, NC.

raised five children, Harriet continued reading and studying subjects of her choice. One of the topics she focused on was the design of houses.

In 1869, when she was forty-one years old, she became the first woman to receive a patent for an architectural innovation. Her patent was for "Improvement in the Construction of Buildings" for the design of a six-sided house. Her house did not have a central hall. A person had to walk through one room to get to another. She designed a heating system that provided heat for all the rooms at once. Harriet thought her design for a house made a more efficient use of space and light. So did her husband and brother-in-law. They formed a company to make and sell the six-sided houses. Harriet and her family lived in one of them. It stood in its original spot in Charlotte, North Carolina, for almost one hundred years.

WHEN AMERICANS SET out to celebrate the country's one hundredth birthday, they decided to have a fair. The 1876 Centennial Exposition in Philadelphia was the first international fair of worldwide importance held in the United States. A Women's Pavilion was created to showcase six hundred exhibits of women's work, as described by Anne L. Macdonald in *Feminine Ingenuity: Women and Invention in America*. Eighty-five female patent holders displayed their inventions in the Women's Pavilion. Fifteen won Centennial Awards. One of them was Elizabeth Stiles, a businesswoman from Philadelphia. What did she display? It was a seven-foot-high reading and writing desk that was folded up when not in use. When it was in use, wooden flaps that were unfolded became writing tables. Racks for newspapers were revealed, as were drawers and shelves for books. She wrote in her 1865 patent that it was for use in "reading rooms, libraries, hotels, steamboats, etcetera." Elizabeth sold her cabinets all over the United States.

At the next United States-based international fair, the World's Columbian Exposition in Chicago in 1893, the organizers attempted to find the unusual by seeking out women inventors. And some of the inventions were truly unusual. One was a sofa bed that could also be a bathtub. Another was a dress stand that could become a fire escape. Another one was a machine most people would like to have had in their homes: a dishwasher. Josephine Cochran's dishwashing machine was not only on display, but it was in use at nearly all the large restaurants of the fair. The Shelbyville, Illinois, woman wrote in her patent of 1886 that she "invented a new and useful improvement in dish-washing Machines. . . . A continuous stream of either soap-suds or clear hot water is supplied to a crate holding the racks . . . holding the dishes while the crate is rotated. . . ." She formed Cochran's Crescent Washing Machine Company to manufacture the dishwasher and sold it to Chicago hotels and restaurants. The price was too high, however, for most people to buy one for their homes.

The creation of another inventor was also in use at the fair. Anyone who visited the Women's Pavilion rode to the second floor in an elevator patented in 1890 by Harriet Tracy of New Brighton, New York. She won the contract to have her elevator installed at the fair. Her concern was safety. Her elevator was designed so as to avoid "injury . . . in case of the . . . too rapid descent of the car." A second patent was for a "safety device for elevators." It allowed those in an elevator to put on the brakes in case the car flew up or down. Harriet was a busy woman.

Thirty years later, Mary Anderson of Birmingham, Alabama, was concerned with the needs of another kind of transportation. Mary was on vacation in New York and decided to tour the city on a streetcar. There was only one problem: bad weather. The streetcar driver had a lot of problems seeing out the window of the car. He stopped

No. 470,960.   Patented Mar. 15, 1892.

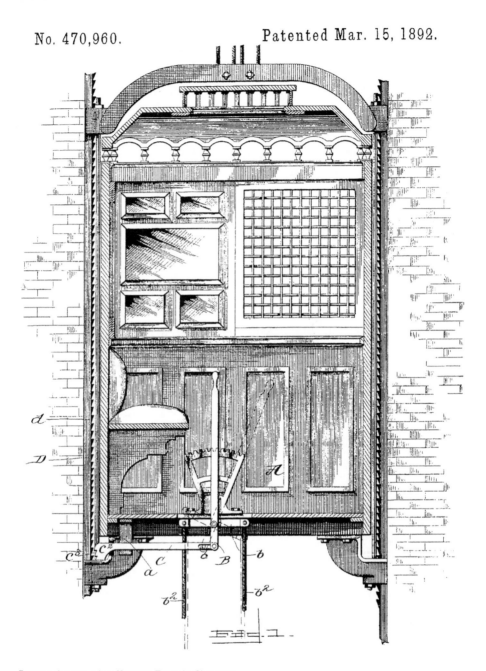

Patent drawing for Harriet Tracy's Elevator.

the streetcar often to clear it off. Mary thought about this, and when she went home, she filed an application for a patent for the windshield wiper. She was granted the patent in 1903. Her design allowed the driver to operate a wiper by hand from inside the bus.

WHAT ABOUT INVENTIONS for children? Sure. In 1872 Jane Wells of Chicago gained a patent for a product that mothers have appreciated ever since: the baby jumper. Forms of the baby jumper are still popular today. Jane's was a stand-alone swing. Once a baby was old enough to sit up, a mother could put her baby in the jumper where it could swing about or bounce on its own. Jane wrote in her patent: "The infant's toes just touch the floor, giving it the ability to dance, swing, and turn itself in any direction."

Some years later, when industrial designer Merry Hull (her real name was Gladys Whitcomb Geissman) of New York became a mother she discovered a problem other mothers already knew about: kids grow out of their clothes too quickly. So, in the 1950s, Merry patented and sold Merry Mites expandable clothing for little ones. In 1986 Nickie and William Campbell patented the Easy to Hold Baby Bottle. It has a hole in the middle of the bottle that makes it easier for babies to hold.

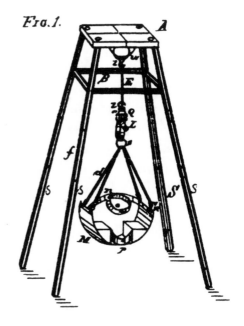

Patent drawing for Jane Wells's Baby Jumper.

Every mother deals with diapers. Did any of them have a better way? Yes. In 1950 Marion Donovan of Saugatuck, Connecticut, gained a patent for a "leakproof diaper." She wrote in her patent application: "Formerly diapers and covers were not leakproof and therefore accessories such as mattress covers, rubber sheets, rubber pants . . . were needed. . . ." Her diapers were sold through a company in Shelbyville, Indiana.

Another woman saw the need for another kind of diaper. While she enjoyed watching her new pet parakeet fly around the house, Bertha L. Dlugi of Milwaukee, Wisconsin, wrote in her 1959 patent application that "a distinct disadvantage . . . is that these birds cannot normally be house trained and their excremental discharge is frequently deposited on household furnishings when they are at liberty. . . ." So she invented a diaper held on by a tiny collar. Bertha claimed that she didn't want the diaper to be annoying to the bird or conspicuous or harmful. She claimed most of it was hidden by feathers.

OTHER WOMEN INVENTED because of educational concerns. Anna Breadin of Philadelphia, most likely a teacher, patented a school desk in 1889. She had a real problem to solve. When students came into the classroom and threw their books and slates onto the wooden desks, it was too noisy! In her patent Anna wrote: "The top of the desk . . . [is] clothed with rubber so that the noise which usually accompanies the throwing of books or slates down on an ordinary desk or the dropping of slates into the slate wells is effectively prevented and the desk is rendered practically noiseless." She added that the "cover cannot . . . be torn or loosened by mischievous scholars." Other women invented aids for teaching music, musical instruments, toys, games, and camping equipment.

Students invent, too. And sometimes their inventions are prompted by a holiday. On Halloween in 1993 someone stole the carved pumpkins right off second grader Emily Strubinger's front porch in Columbus, Ohio. Emily didn't want that to happen again. So she invented the Porch Policeman. It was a button alarm she placed under her pumpkins. If a thief picked up the pumpkin, an alarm would go off. No treats for that thief! Emily entered her invention in a contest and was the regional winner in the Invent America Contest. "The alarm will 100 percent scare the thief away. He will probably put it down and run and will never come to your house again," Emily wrote in her log book.

Alarm of another sort concerned inventor Hedwig Eva Maria Kiesler of Austria, later to be known as actress Hedy Lamarr, star of many Hollywood movies of the 1940s. Living in Vienna just before the start of World War II, she was a film actress and married a rich Austrian armaments manufacturer, Fritz Mandl. She accompanied him to gatherings and listened and suggested ideas when he spoke with his colleagues about arms design and the topic of a radio-controlled torpedo.

In 1938, as the German forces invaded Austria, Hedy decided to flee her country. She eventually moved to Hollywood where she signed a contract with MGM. While she was appearing in films including *Algiers* and *Tortilla Flats*, she read about the outbreak of World War II and wanted to do her part to stop the advance of the German forces. She remembered the discussions about a radio-controlled torpedo and shared her thoughts with George Antheil, a friend who composed music for films.

What might she have explained to him? That the route of a torpedo can be controlled by a radio signal. A transmitter relays commands via the signal. Problems occur when the signal is jammed. Then nothing guides the torpedo. In 1940, during World War II, signals were often jammed. No one had developed a way to prevent it.

That is, until Hedy and George came up with the idea of using frequency hopping. Signals were usually sent on one frequency. Their idea was to send a signal that would hop from one frequency to another rapidly and without a pattern. Since the signal was unpredictable, no one could jam it and interfere with the route of a torpedo.

The two received their patent in August 1942, during World War II, but the military did not use their device during the war. Seventeen years later their patent expired, but the concept they outlined is used widely today in antijamming technology as part of the U.S. government's defense communications satellite system, for wireless Internet transmission, and in cellular phones.

Hedy Lamarr and George Antheil were honored in 1997 for "blazing new trails on the electronic frontier" by the Electronic Frontier Foundation.

$$\geq \bigcirc \leq$$

"AMAZING GRACE" WAS the nickname given to Grace Hopper. Why? Grace was a computer whiz. After she graduated from Yale University, where she studied math and physics, she joined the U.S. Naval Reserve in 1943 as a lieutenant and was sent to the Bureau of Ordinance Computation. She worked there on an early version of the electronic computer, the Mark One. It looked and acted very differently from computers today. To begin with, its dimensions were fifty-one feet long, eight feet high, and five feet wide. Programming the computer to follow the simplest commands involved using a long string of commands made up of a series of the numbers "0" and "1," which might look something like this, only longer: 0011000011111. Programming was a time-consuming process, and it was very easy to make a mistake. Grace saved the day by figuring out a way to talk to the computer in the same language used by people. She programmed the computer to be able to understand commands like "stop" or "go." Her computer language was called COBOL, and it is still used today. In 1984 Grace Hopper became one of six people inducted into the Engineering and Science Hall of Fame. Other inductees include

Thomas Edison, inventor of the lightbulb as well as thousands of other inventions, and Jonas Salk, who developed the polio vaccine. When she retired from the Navy in 1986, she was eighty years old and was the oldest officer on active duty in all of the armed services. She died in 1992 at age eighty-five.

INVENTIONS CAN ALSO be a process, a series of steps that unfold in a new way. What does that mean? W. Jean Dodds of Santa Monica, California, a hematologist, was running the blood bank for the State of New York when she and her team invented and patented a methodology for a more sensitive way to measure blood proteins, not only in humans but also in animals. That means they came up with steps that evolve into a procedure that is new. Her team discovered the common portion of the blood protein in both animals and humans that was preserved through evolutionary development. Then they found a way to measure that protein in all mammals using the same test. Before their discovery and test, scientists had to use different tests for every species, which was costly and time-consuming. Today she runs Hemopet, the only nonprofit blood bank for animals in the United States.

The invention of Dr. Rosalyn Yalow and her partner Dr. Solomon Berson was also a process, a series of steps that evolve in a new way. Many people do not think of a process as an invention, but many patents are granted for processes, especially in the scientific fields. The process, or technique, they developed is Radioimmunoassay, or RIA for short. Their technique uses radioactive isotopes to measure small amounts of biological substances in blood or other bodily fluids. The technique is so sensitive that it can measure a spoonful of sugar in a sixty-mile-long lake. That means that by using RIA, doctors can detect the presence or absence of vitamins, hormones, drugs,

Dr. Rosalyn Yalow in the animal lab. Courtesy of Bronx VA Medical Production Service.

enzymes, viruses, and more. It allows for early detection of many diseases.

When Rosalyn was growing up in the 1920s in the Bronx borough of New York, she was not even ten when she decided she wanted to be a scientist. Her parents taught her to read before she entered kindergarten. By the time she was five, she was making weekly trips to the library with her older brother. In high school math and chemistry were her favorite subjects.

After she graduated from college, Rosalyn wanted to attend graduate school to become a physicist, but she could not do it without financial help. Her parents encouraged her to become an elementary school teacher. Then she was offered a job as a teaching assistant at the University of Illinois at Urbana so she could both work and attend graduate school. On the first day of school she met Aaron Yalow, her future husband.

After gaining her Ph.D., Rosalyn was hired by the Bronx Veterans Hospital, where she spent her professional career. She was interested in studying nuclear medicine and conducting studies related to radioisotopes, but the hospital didn't have a proper space for her. So she set up her own space in what had been the janitor's closet. She later began working with Dr. Solomon Berson. When they first submitted their work on RIA to medical journals, it was turned down. Others didn't accept their discoveries.

Thirty years later, in 1977, Rosalyn was awarded the Nobel Prize in medicine or physiology for the work they did. (Solomon Berson passed away in 1972.) As quoted in *The Lady Laureates*, Rosalyn said in a lecture delivered to the American Association of American Medical Colleges, "We must believe in ourselves or no one else will believe in us; we must match our aspirations with the guts and determination to succeed."

Women inventors are spunky. Like Rosalyn Yalow, many of them have said, "Yes, I can" when others have said, "No, you can't." Womens' inventions contribute to every aspect of life.

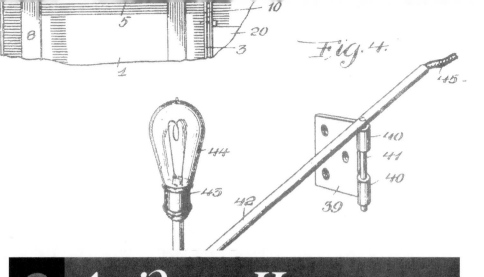

2 Accidents Happen

"If they said it couldn't be done, I'd say, 'Oh, really. . . .' If someone says it can't be done take it as a challenge, not as a discouragement. It's the only way to make inventions."

—Patsy Sherman, coinventor, Scotchgard

*P*atsy Sherman was puzzled. She and Sam Smith, her research partner at 3M Company, were trying to create a synthetic rubber material for fuel hoses for jet aircraft. The existing fuel caused all known rubber products to disintegrate. "We made it in the form of a latex, which is a milky material like the sap of rubber trees from which we get natural rubber," said Patsy. "One day some of the latex accidentally spilled onto the tennis shoe of one of the technicians.

"When it dried nothing could be found to remove it. Not soapy water, or organic solvents, or anything like that. No one had ever thought of a fabric that could repel both oil and water," said Patsy. "So someone got the idea to dip a little piece of fabric in the latex and dry it out. Then we held the fabric under the water. Sure enough, water just bounced right off of it. When we dropped oil on it, it beaded up. Nothing would wet this piece of fabric. We thought maybe there was a better use for this material than for making jet aircraft hoses."

That's how the 3M product Scotchgard was invented in the 1950s—as a result of an accident. Today you can find Scotchgard in any market. It protects material from stains. "The important thing to remember," said Patsy, who has been granted sixteen U.S. patents,

Patsy Sherman and her partner Sam Smith, inventors of Scotchgard, working in the 3M labs. Courtesy of Patsy Sherman.

"is that many of the world's greatest discoveries were unplanned, like penicillin and the vulcanization of rubber. They came about strictly by accident. But somebody was keeping their eyes open and their brain in gear."

"Trust your hunches," said Patsy. "I tell girls, 'We've got a secret weapon called women's intuition.' It's surprising how often it works out."

After the accidental splash on the tennis shoe, Patsy and Sam spent eight years developing the fluorochemical that is known as Scotchgard. There were no known uses for fluorochemicals then. That's why they were experimenting. "We did figure out a way to theoretically design a molecule that would work and also release stain in the laundry," said Patsy. Then they had to make the theory a reality. "Anyone can be an inventor if they just keep their eyes open and question any results that they get," said Patsy. "You have to question anything anybody tells you. If they tell you something can't be done, don't always accept that. If it were that easy to predict what will work and won't work, research scientists could be replaced by a few computers."

Scotchgard became an especially valuable product because of the time in which it was invented. "With the 1960s came the introduction of permanent press fabrics. That cut down on ironing, but if the material was stained it was almost impossible to get the stain out," said Patsy. Scotchgard helped solve that problem. More than thirty products in the Scotchgard line were developed for use on raincoats, carpets, and clothing. After the development of Scotchgard, Patsy worked at 3M Company for many more years and retired in 1992.

$$\Longrightarrow \overset{\displaystyle \bigcirc}{} \Longleftarrow$$

SOME INVENTIONS DO come about as a result of an accident. Inventors are clever because they realize the importance of an accident. Other inventions come about as the result of a plan. But what exactly is an invention? When an inventor applies for a patent, the examiner from the U.S. Patent and Trademark Office asks three questions about an invention: Is it "new"? Is it "useful"? Is it "unobvious"?

Is it "new"? Is it different from what already exists? To be an invention it has to be different from other inventions. It doesn't have to be drastically different, but it must be new in some way. Inventors often try to discover if their idea is original by going to stores that carry similar products. They check in magazines to see if products like theirs are featured in ads or stories.

Is it "useful"? Does anyone need the invention? Could people use it? It doesn't have to be suitable for everyone. It could be useful to people with certain jobs or interests. Could adults or kids use it? Could pet lovers or steelworkers use it? It does not matter who would use it. An invention merely has to be useful. One way to prove it is useful is to sell it. If the inventor sells it or others use it, that can prove that it is useful.

Is it "unobvious"? Is it so obvious that people who are familiar with that type of product would say, "Oh, anyone could figure that out." Then it would not be an invention. An invention is the kind of thing people look at and say, "Why didn't I think of that?"

Is an invention new, useful, and unobvious? Those are the measures of an invention, and women from all walks of life have created inventions. Many of them became inventors as if by accident. They needed something for their careers or daily lives and in creating solutions became inventors.

In the 1890s entertainer Lillian Russell wasn't thinking about becoming an inventor when she was touring the United States as the singing star of musical comedies and light operas. That is, until she became frustrated with trying to find and organize her costumes and cosmetics during her performances. Lillian traveled from town to

Patent drawing of Lillian Russell's Dresser Trunk.

town by train in her own elaborately decorated railroad car, complete with velvet-covered couches. But what about when she got to the theater? Where was a mirror and lights so she could apply her makeup? Where could she keep her costumes? Every theater was different. Lillian wanted to have a makeup table in each place with her makeup and costumes handy.

So she designed a custom dresser trunk she could take with her on the train and have taken to the theater in each town. Once there she opened it up, unfolded several mirrors that were tucked inside, attached electric lights, and presto: it was a well-lit makeup table. Cosmetics were handy in the drawers below, as were the hanging costumes. In 1912 she gained Patent Number 1,014,858 for her trunk. She wrote in her patent application, that it is "a dresser trunk that will answer to the requirements of an actress . . . all the 'makeup' at hand . . . as is necessary when the interval between acts is very short."

Did anyone else use Lillian's dresser trunk? While she designed it for those in the theater, she also thought it could be used "by the traveling public and by campers." It is not known that it was ever produced other than for her own use. But no matter. Lillian was the best-paid performer of her day. And she used it.

$$\geq \widehat{\varphi} \leq$$

LYDIA O'LEARY DIDN'T plan to become an inventor either. She wanted to work in sales in a department store, but no one would hire her. Why? It might have been because she had a red-wine-colored birthmark that covered half of her face. Those doing the job interviews didn't think she should work with the public.

As a girl Lydia spent half her time hiding from her classmates. During recess she hid in the restroom. She hid when other children wanted her to answer their questions about the birthmark. Her parents were concerned and took her to doctors, but none of them had a solution. If they had tried to remove her birthmark her face would have been terribly scarred. She even tried getting a tattoo that matched the color of her skin. That didn't work.

Even though the birthmark was upsetting to Lydia, she set her goals and tried to achieve them. She finished high school and graduated from college. That's when she started applying for jobs in New York City. The only job she was able to get was as a painter of placards. Then one day while she was painting she made a mistake. To fix it she painted over a dark color with several layers of lighter paint. Then she thought about it. Why not cover her birthmark in the same way?

When she tried doing that with makeup available at the stores, it didn't cover her birthmark. She realized that the makeup she needed did not exist. So she went to the corner drugstore, bought some makeup products, and began experimenting with them. She also talked to a chemist. After she concocted a makeup she put it on her face, and it covered her birthmark. Lydia reapplied for a job as a salesperson at the same department store and was hired to work in the hat department. After three weeks she was the top salesperson.

Lydia's life was changed. She told an interviewer for *Reader's Digest* that when she communicated her excitement to her doctor, he encouraged her to share her makeup with others. So she decided to produce it as a product that could be sold in stores. While most foundation makeup is less than 10 percent pigment, Lydia's was 40 percent. That's what made it different. It was specifically designed for people who wanted to cover unattractive marks. When Lydia tried to choose a name for it, she chose one that described the effect: Covermark. One of their ads reads: "Covermark is the original brand of corrective cosmetics from Lydia O'Leary designed to give you the look of a perfect complexion (even if yours is far from it)."

When Lydia applied for a patent she was turned down. The patent examiner did that because the government did not grant patents for cosmetics. Cosmetics were thought of as applications that added to one's beauty. That was the point of Covermark, according to the examiner. Lydia didn't see it that way. Covermark didn't just make her more beautiful. It made it possible for her to function in society. So she appealed.

When Lydia presented her case to the eight judges in the Court of Appeals in Washington, D.C., they refused to give her a patent as well. It was then she realized that the judges did not understand. She asked to be excused. When she returned she had removed her makeup, revealing her face disfigured by the red-wine birthmark. The judges were shocked at the change in her appearance. They realized the value of Covermark — how it could help others with birthmarks or scars. They granted her a patent. She is the one and only person who has ever been granted a patent for a cosmetic.

Lydia started a company to produce and market her product. Although she died in 1957, her company still exists today. Richard Ottaviano, president of Covermark in 1996, remembered seeing Lydia demonstrating her makeup many years ago in a New York department store. "She stripped all the makeup off her face right there in the store," he said, "and she had a few others with birthmarks do the same. She then reapplied her makeup as people watched."

Lydia never forgot her childhood embarrassment about her birthmark. Her company still cares about kids, and, according to Mr. Ottaviano, "If children with birthmarks or other marks contact us, we will provide them with makeup free of charge and with videos that show them how to use it." (Write to Covermark, 202C LaSalle Avenue, Hasbrouch, New Jersey 07604. 1-800-524-1120.)

So Lillian Russell, an actress, and Lydia O'Leary, a saleswoman, became inventors even though they had other careers. That happened to Barbara Thompson, too.

When Barbara Thompson was growing up in Panama City, Florida, she played marathon Monopoly games with her brother and sister. "They thought I was bossy," she said. She thought she was a girl with a mind of her own. "When my parents would tell me to clean the yard one way, I'd clean the yard but do it another way. What could they say?"

So what did Barbara do as an adult? She studied and became a teacher. After working as one for five years, she began studying for a doctorate in Education and Computer Science at North Texas State University. She thought there might be a way to use computers to help children learn, and she talked about this idea to her professors at school. A company nearby, Texas Instruments, had developed a voice chip that made it possible for computers to talk. They wanted to use that technology to help kids learn. But how? That's where Barbara came in. She worked with Texas Instruments to develop learning tools and toys including Touch and Tell and Speak and Read.

How does Touch and Tell work? A child touches a picture of an animal, and the voice chip in the toy says the name of the animal. With Speak and Read kids push a button, hear a word, and see it on a screen.

Barbara worked with other companies after leaving Texas Instruments and started her own company to manufacture other learning tools including Tutor Clock and Tutor Money Machine to teach kids time, money, and math skills. Today Barbara has a company, Innovation Resources, that helps inventors market their products. She is an inventor or codeveloper on nine patents.

On the other side of the world, another woman with a full life was thinking of an idea that would turn her into an inventor, as described by Farag Moussa in *Women Inventors*. In Sydney, Australia, Joan Stuckey, a wife and mother, found herself with extra time when her children grew up. She thought about the problems of people confined to their beds—that they develop bed sores at pressure points like their heels, shoulders, or hips. Why? Because the blood can't circulate and the sores can't heal with the continued pressure. She tried to think of a solution and one day thought of the principle discovered in the seventeenth century by French philosopher and scientist Blaise Pascal. The principle was that if you have a flexible container and it contains fluid, when you apply pressure to the outside of it, the pressure is equal in all directions.

Using that principle Joan created a mattress cover, a seat cushion, and an exercise cushion. When a person lies in bed on one of Joan's mattress covers or sits on one of her seat cushions his or her weight is evenly distributed. The way that the cushion is made prevents aggravation or strain on the pressure points. She created a company to market her product, Push Cush, and sells it all over Australia and in Japan.

So an actress, a saleswoman, a teacher, and a homemaker became inventors. Other women inventors have been involved in almost every business or activity. Sometimes it is not that they want to become inventors but that they are forced to become inventors just to solve their financial problems. That's what happened to Harriet Strong.

Harriet Strong was thirty-nine years old and living on a farm in the Whittier area of Southern California with Charles, her husband of twenty years, and their four children. She was in poor health, and becoming an inventor never entered her mind. Then Charles committed suicide. It was 1883, and he had lost the family fortune in a silver-mining scam.

What happened? Harriet studied agriculture and her health improved. She wanted to know what crops grew well in her area, and after much study she chose to grow walnuts. Ten years later she was known as the Walnut Queen. Her orchard became the largest one in the world. It was twenty-five miles long. She was the first farmer to introduce winter irrigation of the crop. Later she also grew citrus fruits, pomegranates, and pampas grass.

How did Harriet become an inventor? When lack of water threatened to ruin her first harvest, she designed and patented a flood con-

Harriet Strong. Courtesy of the Whittier Historical Society, Whittier, CA.

trol/storage dam system. The system was unique in that it incorporated a succession of dams that ensured safety in case of a break, utilizing the pressure of the water itself for structural support of the preceding dam and regulating water in a controlled, uniform manner.

All her accomplishments did not go unnoticed. She was the first woman elected to the Los Angeles Chamber of Commerce and the first president of the Business League of America. When the government was considering development of the Colorado River, she was called before Congress to give expert testimony. She gained national attention at the World's Columbian Exposition in Chicago in 1893. She also received an award from the Federal Agricultural and Mining Department.

SOMETIMES AN INVENTOR is called on to use her inventive skills to create an invention for others. In Lillian Greneker's case, she was asked to help with efforts to fight World War II.

Artist Lillian Greneker was running Greneker Corporation, a successful business in Pleasantville, New York, that produced flexible mannequins of cellophane or paper. At her factory she was approached by businessmen from U.S. Rubber, the company making the rubber fuel tanks for navy planes and submarines. The fuel tanks were made by gluing and vulcanizing sheets of rubber over a form — forms like her mannequins.

What was their problem? They needed to remove the form once the tank was completed. Those at U.S. Rubber had overseen many experiments to try to solve this problem themselves. They had tried many materials, including plaster, but none had worked. Since Lillian's mannequins were made of paper they thought she might be able to create a mold out of paper that would be easy to remove. They presented the problem to Lillian. She, too, thought of plaster as the solution. Even though they disagreed, Lillian tried the plaster, conducting an experiment in a new way with one of her mannequins. She used a combination of plaster and rope. It was a simple and effective solution. When the plaster dried, someone had only to pull the rope to pull apart the plaster without damaging the tank. She gained three patents for her Pullcord, which was used in the war effort.

Lillian's interests as an artist later led her to invent and patent Fingertips, attachments for fingers that held small paint brushes. An artist could have five brushes on each hand, each with a different color paint. Lillian got another patent that improved on Fingertips when she was eighty-five years old. She died in 1990 at age ninety-five.

INVENTORS DON'T ALWAYS have to invent something completely new. They can improve on something that already exists. Think about familiar items that are always being improved: bicycles, televisions, radios, toothbrushes. That is called innovation. Innovation is a type of invention. It is new because it improves the old version. It is still useful. That makes an innovation an invention.

One product had an innovation before it was ever sold in the stores. That product was Bounce, the antistatic tissue for the dryer. It was invented by a California chemist named Conrad Gaiser. He and his wife, Audrey, lived in Long Beach on the third floor of an apartment building. Conrad noticed her trying to determine when to go down to the first floor laundry room to add the liquid softener to the wash. He thought, "There ought to be a softener you could throw in the dryer." And he developed Bounce and sold it to Procter & Gamble. They hired him to help test and improve Bounce so it could be sold as a product. They tested it by throwing it in with wet laundry. What laundry? That's just it. At Procter & Gamble employees brought in their family laundry, and the company tested their products on it. So some of the employees did the laundry. One of them was a laundress named Agnes Mcqueary.

Agnes watched as Conrad and other scientists tested Bounce. She was aware of one of the problems: if there was too small a load in the dryer, the tissue would sometimes stick to and block the air outlet. That caused the dryer to overheat and automatically turn off. The clothes would not get dry. Agnes took some of the Bounce tissues home with her, placed them on a surface, and with a kitchen knife cut slits in the middle of the tissue. The slits allowed the air to flow through the tissue. It worked. Agnes's modification of Bounce improved it. What she did is called an innovation. She gained a patent in her name for her improvement, her innovation.

Many inventions come about as a result of observation. Others are created as a result of accidents. Others are planned. Whatever the origin, inventions are needed for every area of life. That means that there is a need for inventors in every area of life.

Activity A SCOTCHGARD EXPERIMENT

Patsy Sherman offered the following experiment for you to do at home. It's one she and Sam Smith often did when they wanted to explain the properties of Scotchgard to business executives and other groups of people.

Materials
1 piece of cardboard, one foot square, with your initials or some other shape cut out
2 pieces of spare fabric, one foot square
1 can of Scotchgard
A hot iron and an ironing board
1 cup of water in a bowl
1 cup of oil in a different bowl

Procedure

Lay the cardboard stencil over the fabric pieces. Thoroughly spray the area revealed by the stencil with the fluorochemical Scotchgard. Cover the area well with the Scotchgard. Then let it dry. Iron each piece of fabric so that you have a good film around each little fiber. Ironing makes the Scotchgard penetrate. Then dip one piece of fabric in the bowl of water and the other piece of fabric in the bowl of oil.

Observations

When you hold up the pieces of fabric, every part of the fabric will be wet or oily except the area coated with Scotchgard! It's your own Scotchgard experiment—a way to see that Scotchgard really does protect against water and oil penetration.

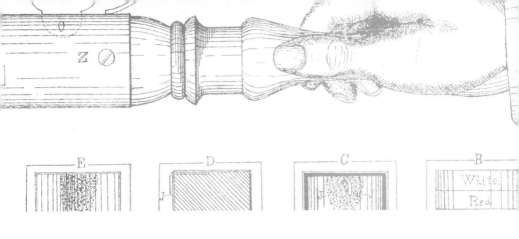

3 *Turning an Idea into a Model*

"I was thinking that I want to play a game with my friends and this sounds like fun but it doesn't exist so maybe I could make it. The best inventions come out of that situation."

—*Patty Brandetsas, inventor, Whirling Dart Board*

aria Telkes was fascinated with the sun. When she was in high school in Budapest, Hungary, she started reading about it. When she finished reading everything written in Hungarian, she started reading what was written in French, English, and German.

Is it any wonder that she designed a system for solar heating a home?

After Maria gained a Ph.D. in physical chemistry from the University of Budapest, she traveled to the United States in 1925 to visit a relative and eventually joined the Massachusetts Institute of Technology Solar Energy Research Project. While she was there, a Boston sculptor, Amelia Peabody, approached Maria and offered to pay for the construction of a solar-heated house on land she owned in Dover, Massachusetts. The house was to be designed by architect

Eleanor Raymond. Maria was to design the solar-heating system. That was in 1948.

While other solar-energy systems relied on heating water or rocks, Maria devised a system using a chemical that would last indefinitely that crystallized and retained the heat. That heat then kept the five-room house warm throughout the winter. Maria gained several patents for her system of storing solar heat.

"I envisage the day when solar heat collecting shelters, like power stations, will be built apart from the house," she told W. Clifford Harvey of the *Christian Science Monitor*. "One such solar-heating building could develop enough heat from the sun for pumping into an entire community of homes."

Maria continued working in solar-energy research at various American universities and corporations. She experimented with solar ovens that could be used by villagers who live in dry areas that don't have many trees or other materials that can be used as heating fuel. She developed a "solar still" for the U.S. Navy in World War II. It could be installed in life rafts to turn salt water into drinking water and saved the lives of many pilots whose planes were shot down and sailors whose boats were torpedoed. She died at age ninety-five on her first visit to her native Hungary in seventy years.

In the 1870s, Mary Nolan, a magazine editor and publisher who lived and worked in St. Louis, was thinking of another aspect of the home when she invented a hollow, fireproof brick that could be used as a building material. Mary's father was a contractor, so as she grew up she learned about the building trade. She wanted to create a brick that was fireproof and fit together with interlocking parts. She spent years experimenting in order to create a brick she called Nolanum. The bricks could fit together to make a wall. In her patent application, called "Improvement in Building Blocks," she wrote "the blocks are so intimately connected together that the wall will present a . . . finished appearance, so as to render the use of plaster unnecessary. . . ."

She received a special award at the 1876 Centennial Exposition in Philadelphia, the fair celebrating the one hundredth anniversary of the United States.

Mary Nolan wanted to build a wall without plaster. At about the same time Mary Potts created an invention made of plaster. Mary Potts lived in the time before wrinkle-free clothing when people spent a lot of time ironing. And they had a variety of irons — ones for ruffles, others for sheets, others for ordinary items.

Irons were very heavy back then because they were made entirely of iron. They were called "sad irons" because the word *sad* meant heavy. Because Mary lived before the invention of electricity, she and others heated the irons by placing them on a stove, as described in *From Indian Corn to Outer Space: Women Invent in America* by Ellen H. Showell and Fred M. B. Amram. Usually they heated several irons at once. The problem was that while the iron was heating up enough to iron the clothing, the iron handle was heating up as well. Mary would have used a cloth to hold it. Still, it was tricky. She would have had to wait for the iron to cool down enough

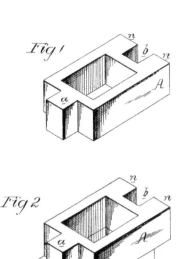

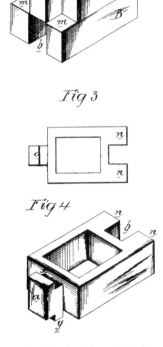

MARY NOLAN.
BUILDING-BLOCKS.

Patent drawing for Mary Nolan's Building Blocks.

so that the heat radiating off it wouldn't burn her hand. Then again, the iron had to be hot enough to remove the wrinkles from the clothes.

Mary wanted to do something to make ironing easier. Because her father was a plasterer, Mary knew a lot about plaster. It occurred to her that if an iron were made of plaster and covered with a thin layer of iron it would be much lighter and much cooler. Plaster would not retain heat as iron did. So Mary made a model based on her idea. It had a wooden handle that was much easier to hold. The handle was also detachable. Why was that important? As Mary would heat several irons on the stove, she would attach the handle to one of them when it reached the right temperature. Then she would use that for ironing. When the iron became too cool to use, Mary would place the iron back on the stove, detach the handle, and then attach the handle to another iron—a hot one. And on and on. Mary patented her iron in 1870 and sold her idea to American Enterprise Manufacturing Company; her product was used all over America by the end of the 1800s. It was called Mrs. Potts's Sad Iron.

Maria Telkes, Mary Nolan, and Mary Potts all made models of their inventions. A model allows an inventor to see that an idea works. It is a crucial aspect of inventing. If the model doesn't work, they may discover they've used the wrong materials. They may have to experiment with many different materials before finding the right ones. Inventors may have to experiment with the way an invention works. Perhaps a switch doesn't work. Or a process is too complicated. If the invention needs to be heated, perhaps it was heated at the wrong temperature or for the wrong amount of time. As inventors make working models they must constantly solve problems.

WHEN PATTY BRANDETSAS first thought of her idea for a Whirling Dart Board, she was an eighth grader in Mary Kincaid's class at

Alexander Graham Middle School in Charlotte, North Carolina. Her idea was to make a dart game a bit more fun. Make it turn. Make it more of a challenge. So she took an ordinary dart board and attached a battery device so that the board would turn as the player threw the darts; that's where her problems started. She used regular batteries at first, and the board spun so fast that it almost broke. "It was hard to get it to the right speed," said Patty. "I used different levels of batteries and my teacher had an adapter to get the motor going at the right speed." What did she do? After experimenting with lots of batteries she found a solution. "I ended up using two AA batteries that were very low on juice. Anything else would make it spin too fast." Patty was the 1995 fourth-place finisher in the Duracell USA competition.

While Patty knew to focus on the batteries, many inventors may not know what aspect of their invention is creating the problem. That's why testing an invention can be involving. That was Martha Coston's situation when she saw inventing as a solution to the problems she faced.

In the mid-1800s, however, Martha wasn't thinking about testing or inventing. She was happily married and busy raising her children. She was only fourteen when she met her future husband, Benjamin Coston. He was sixteen. Two years later they were married. He was an inventor who worked in a research laboratory in Washington, D.C., and was recognized by the U.S. Navy for his inventions. One of the projects Benjamin worked on for the Navy was signal flares that could be used to let people know the location of a ship at sea.

Benjamin and Martha had an active social life in Washington. Among their friends were well-known Americans including Daniel Webster, First Lady Dolley Madison, and John Quincy Adams. Then Benjamin came down with pneumonia. Several months later he was dead. He was only twenty-six.

Martha was in a tough spot. She had very little money to raise her four children. Then one day, as she was looking through Benjamin's

MARTHA J. COSTON.

Improvement in Pyrotechnic Night Signals.

Patented June 13, 1871.

No. 115,935.

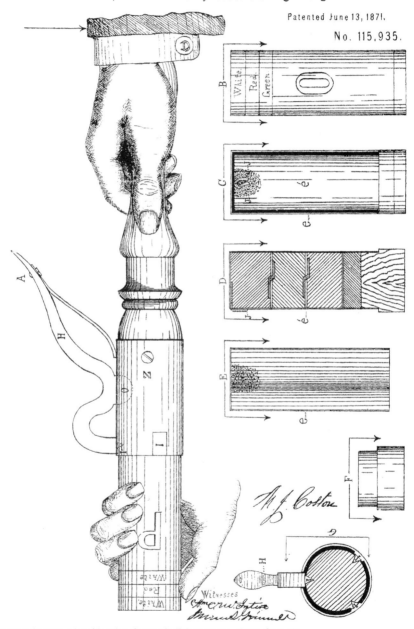

Patent drawing for Martha Coston's Telegraphic Night Signals.

things, she found the plans for the signal flares. She thought that if she could make and sell them she could support her family. She sent to the U.S. Navy for Benjamin's models of the flares, but when she received them she was disappointed. Benjamin had designed them, but he had not finished perfecting his working models. His idea was a good one. The problem: the flares didn't work.

Martha tried to make them work. She wanted the flares to light up in different colors: red, white, and blue. But she wasn't successful either. Then she went to a fireworks show. As she watched the lights explode in the sky she thought that the people who made fireworks might know how to finish the flares. So she met and worked with them and then was able to create red, white, and green flares. When she gained a patent John Quincy Adams was one of her witnesses.

Martha sold Coston Telegraphic Night Signals to the U.S. government for use during the Civil War. Since the flares burned in different colors, they allowed ships to signal one another in fog, in dark, or over distance. They helped prevent shipwrecks. They were used to help locate people who were lost at sea.

Martha eventually got patents in England, France, Holland, Austria, Denmark, Italy, and Sweden. In her later years she traveled widely throughout Europe, including Russia and Scandinavia. She never remarried.

MAKING A MODEL or prototype work means solving lots of problems, as Martha Coston did. Because inventions are so varied, testing has many definitions. Carrie Everson's invention involved a process, a way of doing something, so tests for her were of a different sort.

Carrie Everson was a curious person even before she became the wife of Dr. W. K. Everson of Chicago. Because he was a physician, druggist, and chemist, Carrie learned about medicine and chemistry.

When he invested money in mining ventures in Colorado and Mexico, she began experimenting with metals including gold, silver, and copper. She wanted to devise a way to efficiently separate the precious metals from the waste material. There must be a way, she thought. When her husband lost his fortune and subsequently died, she began working as a nurse to support herself and her infant son. She looked to her experiments as an alternative means of support.

Carrie ground ore by hand and examined it under a microscope and made a discovery. Her discovery was that the precious metals in the ore like gold or silver would unite with compounds of fats and acids, but the other rock materials in the ore would not. Her invention, as she wrote in her patent application in 1885, "consists in commingling with pulverized ore a fat or an oil, washing out the non-precious rock with water containing an acid." She continued, "The mineral may be roasted . . . the oil will burn out and the acid will be eliminated." This was an improvement on the methods of recovering ore that were used at that time. "I have used petroleum . . . also tallow, lard, cotton-seed oil, castor oil, and linseed oil. The acids which I have employed are sulphuric, hydrochloric, nitric, phosphoric, acetic, oxalic, tannic, and gallic."

While Carrie was not successful in interesting mining companies in her methods—so much ore was readily available then—she did convince the patent examiner that her invention was new, useful, and unobvious.

Inventors like Martha Coston and Carrie Everson keep track of their progress by recording information in a log. In the log they can jot down their ideas for inventions, drawings of those inventions, notes on research they do, and interviews with people about the invention. They can write about their experiments and tests. They can write down problems they are having. Or list materials they want to use or buy.

Logs usually include the date and time of work. Some logs are neat. Others are messy. The important aspect of a log is the recording of the information. Inventors usually write in ink so that none of their notes can be erased. If they make a mistake they cross it out and put their initials and the date next to the mistake. Why? So that they show all their work, even the mistakes. The result is that they have a record of *what* they did and *when* in case they need proof.

Inventors usually ask others to witness their work. Witnesses read logs or pages of logs then sign their names and give the date as proof that they were witnesses to an inventor's work. A log is evidence. The signatures by witnesses prove when an inventor did certain experiments.

Why all the rules? Inventions are valuable. A log is a record of an inventor's work and ideas. It helps inventors explain their work when they are finished. It helps them prove that they thought of an invention in case someone doubts them.

Many inventors have had to prove that they invented a product. Margaret Knight was one of them. In the late 1860s Margaret Knight was working in a factory in Springfield, Massachusetts, that manufactured paper bags. After watching and working on a paper-feeding machine, she thought of a way to improve on it so that it would fold square-bottomed bags. Presto! The grocery bag. She talked to her boss, who thought it was a good idea. He allowed her to make a wooden model of her idea for a machine. She tested it for a year in the factory.

When Margaret was satisfied with the performance of her machine, she wanted to have it manufactured in metal. So she went to a machinist. Because she created the design and plan of the machine, she was the inventor. It was the job of the machinist to follow her plans and manufacture the machine.

After the machinist had completed the metal model of Margaret's paper bag folding machine, she wanted to establish that she was the

Margaret Knight's Paper Bag Folding Machine. Courtesy of the Smithsonian Institution.

inventor by applying for a patent. When she did, the patent examiner told her that someone else had already invented the machine. She was surprised because she thought she would have heard of a machine similar to hers.

When she did some detective work, she discovered that a man at the machine shop, a Charles F. Annan, had seen her machine and applied for a patent in his name. He claimed the machine was his invention. He received the patent. That's why Margaret was turned down.

What did Margaret have to do? She had to prove she was the real inventor. She hired a lawyer to help her fight for the patent. She testified and brought forth witnesses including the employer that allowed her to test the machine. She presented her drawings and other evidence of her ideas. The judge ruled that the patent should be taken away from the man and given to Margaret. It was granted to her in 1870 when she was thirty-two. Later she and a partner started a company to manufacture paper bags.

The Paper Bag Folding Machine was not her first invention. Margaret started when she was a girl growing up in the 1840s and 1850s in York, Maine. That was in the years before the airplane, television, radio, or computer were invented, and Margaret created her own toys. "I was famous for my kites, and my sleds were the envy and admiration of all the boys in town," she once said. It bothered her somewhat that she was not like other girls, but she concluded that "I couldn't help it, and sought further consolation from my tools."

She was unusual in that so many of her inventions concerned machinery. And she certainly was adept. Once, while she was only twelve, she was visiting her brothers where they worked at a cotton mill. When she witnessed an accident, she invented a solution. She saw a shuttle on one of the looms come loose and hurt a nearby worker. That bothered her. So she invented a safety device that would stop the machine if any other shuttles came loose.

In her lifetime Margaret received twenty-seven patents including one for a rotary engine, one for window sashes, and one for a machine that cut and sewed shoes. She gained her last patent when she was seventy-four years old, and she lived to be seventy-six.

$$\gtrless \bigodot \lessgtr$$

WHEN INVENTORS START to make models, access to materials is an important consideration. Mary Nolan was able to make construction bricks because her father was a contractor. Mary Potts had access to plaster because her father was a plasterer. Margaret Knight was able to test the paper bag folding machine because she worked in the paper bag factory.

What if an inventor is good at thinking of ideas but not so good at making models? That's when inventors with ideas find a machinist, craftsperson, or other type of model maker who will craft their invention. To protect themselves most inventors ask the model makers to sign a nondisclosure agreement. That means they agree not to tell others about the invention or to make it for themselves.

Beulah Henry, the most prolific woman inventor of the 1920s, was called "Lady Edison" because of her forty-five patents. She successfully used model makers in creating her inventions. "I get a complete picture in my mind of what the invention will be like when it is finished and then set to work to get my model maker to create a model to fit my mind's picture," she told a reporter. "Inventing is really easy; it's the development work that is heart-breaking."

She told another reporter, "I know nothing about mechanical terms and am afraid I do make it rather difficult for the draughtsmen to whom I explain my ideas, but in the factories where I am known they are exceedingly patient with me because they seem to have a lot of faith in my inventiveness."

But in fact Beulah did know something about mechanics. She had to. When she wanted to create an umbrella with snap-on covers to match a person's outfit, she couldn't find a manufacturer who would take on the task. "It won't work," one after another told her. "A good wind would blow it off." That's when Beulah set out to prove them wrong. She got out some household tools and created an umbrella with removable covers. Once she had the working model, she found a manufacturer that would produce it according to her methods. Beulah, who was known not only for her cleverness but for her movie star-like appearance, sold the fashionable umbrella to New York's best department stores where it was displayed in the windows.

Beulah, a descendent of the patriot Patrick Henry, started her inventing career at age fifteen when she patented a vacuum ice-cream freezer. Her other inventions were ones for the ordinary consumer. Her telephone index attached to a phone and opened like a fan. Her kiddie clock helped kids learn the time of day. Interchangeable snap-on wigs transformed her Miss Illusion Doll from a blond to a brunette. By pushing a button, a person could change the doll's eyes from blue to brown. Have you ever had a problem holding on to a bar of soap in the tub? Beulah thought of a solution. Her Takes the Cake doll-shaped rubber sponge had the soap snapped into the center so it couldn't slip. Her favorite invention, and one of her most profitable, was a plush toy cow that moos and gives milk from a rubber udder. She called it the Milka-Moo.

Beulah continued to patent until the 1960s. One later invention was a typewriter attachment that gave four original copies without carbon paper. In 1962 she gained her forty-fifth patent for a combination mailing and return envelope that can be manufactured in continuous strips. She sold most of her inventions and supported herself from the sales, as reported in a 1962 article in the *New York Times*.

Although she grew up in North Carolina, Beulah lived most of her adult life in hotels in New York. The Seville Hotel was her home for many years, where she lived with a parakeet, two doves, two turtles, and two cockatiels, Genevieve and Baby Audubon.

One way that Beulah had fun with her inventions was in choosing their names. She chose catchy names for her inventions like "Milka-Moo" for her toy cow. The "Miss Illusion Doll" was named for its charm—that its appearance could change. Other inventors named their inventions after themselves. Mrs. Potts did when she named her invention "Mrs. Potts's Sad Iron." Mary Nolan named her construction brick after herself too: "Nolanum." Martha Coston used her name and a description of her invention in its name: "Coston Telegraphic Night Signals." Patty Brandetsas named hers after what it did: "Whirling Dart Board."

INVENTORS MAKE MANY decisions in the process of inventing. From thinking of the idea and making it work to testing it and naming it, inventions are the result of many changes and decisions and creative thoughts. When inventors start to make a model, they have to consider cost. Can they afford to make a model of their idea? It would be less expensive to make a model of an iron than of a solar-heated house. Another consideration is safety. Is it safe to make? Is it safe for the user? What is its effect on the environment? Will it destroy, pollute, or help the environment? Creating a model is a challenging task.

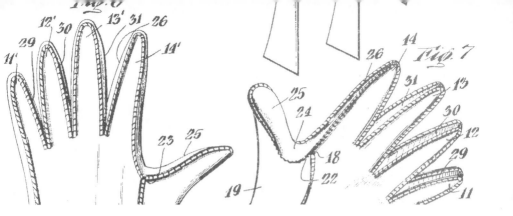

4 *Awards Bring Recognition*

"I never let myself be discouraged if things went wrong. You can't let a few failures dissuade you from your purpose."

— Gertrude Elion, Nobel Prize winner, 1988

When Gertrude Elion was a little girl she often went to the park with her grandfather. After she played, he would tell her stories of his life growing up in Russia. Spending time with him was an important part of her early life. That's why it affected her so deeply when her grandfather became sick. She was fifteen and about to graduate from high school. Soon after, he died a painful death from cancer. "It made a terrific impression on me because we'd been so close," said Gertrude. "I decided then to become a scientist and work in cancer research."

Twenty years later she and her research partner, Dr. George Hitchings, developed drugs that fight childhood leukemia, a type of cancer. "One usually doesn't think of drugs as an invention," said Gertrude, "but they are."

Gertrude was thirty-two in 1950 when she and Dr. Hitchings got their first patent. They worked at Burroughs-Wellcome Company

Gertrude Elion. Courtesy of Glaxo Wellcome Inc.

where they were granted more than forty patents for their research, including one for a drug that makes it possible for people to have kidney transplants. Their research also led to the discovery of AZT, which helps AIDS patients. In 1988 they were awarded the Nobel Prize in medicine or physiology.

Gertrude had to solve many problems on the way to achieving her goals. When she graduated from New York's Hunter College in 1937 with the highest honors, she was not able to afford to go on to graduate school because her family had suffered financial losses during the Depression. So when she applied to fifteen graduate schools, she decided to ask for financial aid. She was turned down by all of them. So she applied for work as a scientific researcher in different laboratories. Again, she was turned down by all of them. One interviewer told her that it was because she was a woman — she might distract the men.

While she lived at home with her parents, Gertrude worked as a high school teacher and attended classes at night toward a masters degree in chemistry at New York University. To increase her chances of one day working in a laboratory, she volunteered in one in order to get experience.

Gertrude's chance to finally work as a chemist came during World War II when many of the male chemists were away. There was a need for chemists. She first worked in a food laboratory and later in a research laboratory. In the mid-1940s she joined the Burroughs-Wellcome Company, where she stayed until she retired.

In March of 1991 Gertrude Elion was the first woman inducted into the National Inventors Hall of Fame. She said, "I'm happy to be the first woman, but I doubt I'll be the last."

And she wasn't. Since then three other women have been inducted into the National Inventors Hall of Fame. It was established in 1973 by the National Council of Intellectual Property Law Association and the U.S. Patent and Trademark Office. It is housed in Inventure Place in Akron, Ohio. The 120 inventors who were initially inducted include Thomas Edison, inventor of the electric lightbulb and the phonograph; Alexander Graham Bell, inventor of the telephone; and Orville and Wilbur Wright, inventors of the first practical powered airplane capable of flight.

In 1994 Elizabeth Lee Hazen and Rachel Fuller Brown became the second and third women inducted into the National Inventors Hall of Fame. They developed Nystatin, the world's first antifungal antibiotic. It was introduced in 1954 and is used to cure fungal infections like ringworm and other diseases of the skin, mouth, throat, and intestinal tract. It is also used by horticulturists to treat Dutch elm disease in trees. It has an artistic use, too. When mold threatened to destroy water-damaged works of art after floods in Italy, Nystatin was used in the restoration. And companies shipping bananas spray the fruit with Nystatin so that the fruit does not get moldy during the trip.

Elizabeth and Rachel met because they were both interested in fungi. *Fungi* is the name of a group of simple plants. There are 250,000 kinds of fungi that occur in air, soil, and water. Some are too small to be seen with the eye; others grow to be several feet wide or high. Fungi can destroy plants or trees and cause disease in humans.

Elizabeth Hazen (left) and Rachel Brown working in the laboratory in 1955. Courtesy of the New York State Department of Health.

When antibiotics like penicillin were discovered in the 1940s, they killed bacteria but they also killed microorganisms controlling the growth of fungi. That meant that fungi, including harmful ones, were growing rapidly. While many substances were created to kill fungi, they could also kill people. That's why scientists were eager to find a substance to kill only harmful fungi.

In 1948 Elizabeth and Rachel were both working on the development of fungicides for the New York State Department of Health. Elizabeth was in New York City, and Rachel was in Albany, New York. Because they were both interested in fungi, they began sharing the results of their studies by mail.

To develop a fungicide to destroy or stop the growth of fungi that caused disease, Elizabeth and Rachel needed to find organisms growing in dirt or soil that would naturally fight the fungi. Once they did that, they could create a substance in the laboratory that would do the same. How did they do their research? In the laboratory Rachel would make cultures of bacteria found in dirt or soil samples they had analyzed. They collected the dirt from many different places but couldn't find the organism they needed. Then, while Elizabeth was on vacation in Virginia, she decided to collect a clump of soil from a local farmer's cow pasture. What a souvenir! But when that soil was analyzed in the lab, the two scientists found an organism they needed to create an antifungal antibiotic. Elizabeth and Rachel decided to name it "Nystatin." The name is a combination of the letters in the name of the laboratory where they worked: New York State Department of Health.

They made another decision: to donate the profits of the invention to fund research and scholarship. They applied for a patent through the nonprofit Research Corporation, which licensed E. R. Squibb to manufacture Nystatin. Since 1948, more than thirteen million dollars has gone into the research and scholarship funds for college and university students.

IN 1995 STEPHANIE KWOLEK was the fourth woman inducted into the National Inventors Hall of Fame. She invented Kevlar, a polymer fiber thread, five times stronger than the same weight of steel. It is used to make bulletproof vests, canoes, skis, and radial tires.

When Stephanie began working as a chemist at DuPont Laboratories in 1946, she actually wanted to be in medical school studying to become a doctor, but she didn't have enough money. "I joined DuPont as a temporary measure," she once said, "but the work turned out to be so interesting that I stayed on."

She began her work at a time when chemists were creating synthetic fibers. Cotton and silk are examples of natural fibers, but they have limitations. They wrinkle and absorb stains easily. Many companies wanted their chemists to create synthetic fibers. In 1939 nylon, one synthetic fiber, was created. Dacron polyester, another synthetic fiber, was created about the same time. Clothes made out of Dacron are often wrinkle-free.

As Stephanie began her job, she was asked to try to create a strong, tough fiber. When she created Kevlar, she discovered it would not rust, was lighter than asbestos, and was stronger than steel. Kevlar is now used to make aircraft ropes that keep floating oil platforms attached to the ocean bottom, protective gloves for woodcutters, and many other items.

Stephanie was surprised when she invented Kevlar because she did her experiments in an unusual way. "I had the results a number of times before I told anyone," she said. "They were so unusual, I didn't want to be embarrassed if they were incorrect."

Stephanie got a patent for Kevlar in 1971 and assigned it to her company, DuPont. She also was granted twenty-seven other patents. She is now retired but still works as a consultant for DuPont.

IT'S NOT JUST American women who are inventing. Women all over the world are inventing products that help fight disease or improve peoples' lives. In 1979 the World Intellectual Property Organization (WIPO) began recognizing women inventors by giving them Gold Medal Awards, as reported by Farag Moussa in *Women Inventors*.

Luce Pince My received her Gold Medal in 1988 for her invention of an A.M.-P.M. watch. In her work as an airline stewardess, she was constantly resetting her watch as she traveled around the world. While she began her efforts to design a time-difference watch, she changed directions and started to develop one that enables the wearer to distinguish ante-meridiem from post-meridiem time. It is white during the day and becomes gradually darker as night falls.

Aino Heikkinen of Finland was honored as an Outstanding Finnish Inventor and received the WIPO Award in 1990. Aino works as an engineer. When she joined 1,400 others working in manufacturing at Lujabetoni Company in Finland, she was presented with a challenge: come up with a cheaper way to make concrete.

What did she know about concrete? That it was made from sand, gravel, cement, and water. Cement is the most expensive ingredient. She discovered that if she reduced the amount of cement and added blast-furnace slag grain, the two would bond and form a cheaper concrete that was also strong and durable. The cheaper element has been produced by the company.

WIPO also recognizes young inventors who are honored in their own countries.

The Youth Science Foundation of Canada has sponsored an annual Canada-wide Science Fair since 1962. In 1987 Anita Luszszak of Alberta, Canada, received a WIPO Gold Medal and first place at the first International Science Fair, held in Quebec. In her project "The Pulsating Generator" she studied the efficiency of electrical generators governed by a pulsing exciter and found they produced more power with less energy, a fact that is potentially valuable to electrical power companies.

In China, a national contest for young inventors is hosted every two years. In 1986 the highest honor and WIPO Award went to thirteen-year-old Liu Hongyan of Lanzhou, China. Her invention was a mathematical fan that is an illustration of complicated mathematical principles.

In 1985 Korea hosted the National Excellent Inventions Exhibition of Korea, called "NIEX 1985." One of the awards went to In-Soon Park, a high school student at Jang Sung, an agricultural village. WIPO then granted her a prize as well for her new type of gardening hoe. It has a double blade. One side is for taking out the surface weeds, the other side is for taking out the deep-rooted ones. Her hoe makes it possible to garden and hoe at the same time.

In America schools, companies, states, and the federal government are encouraging young people to invent while they are still in school.

Everyone wins in an invention contest. Why? After the contest is over, inventors still have their inventions. An invention is property. Inventors can enter other contests or apply for patents. They can sell their inventions as products.

Many students enter a variety of contests. Both kindergartner Emily Giles and her sister, first-grader Molly Giles, of Frederick Law Olmstead school in Buffalo, New York, entered the school invention program in the late 1980s. Molly won in her grade for her Car Desk. It was a type of tray with an elastic strap to hold paper, a cupholder, and pockets for crayons and pencils. "When we went on vacation," said Molly, "we always wanted to color and never had anything to write on." Emily won for the kindergarten class with her Kids' Fire Escape. She got the idea for it after a fireman talked at her school.

He told her class how important it is to get out of a burning room. "I thought, 'What if it was in the middle of the night and you couldn't see anything?'" said Emily. So she came up with the idea of glow-in-the-dark teddy bear feet that would lead the way from her bed to the door.

After Emily won at her school, her teacher entered her invention into the countywide competition. She didn't win. Then her invention was entered in the statewide contest, and it won first place in the state. Many students do just that. If they don't win one contest, they enter another.

Student inventors who are winners in their state can enter their inventions in national contests. Molly Hogan entered the competition at her school in Torrington, Connecticut, and won. Her teacher, Rick Fasciano, submitted her invention to the Young Inventors and

Molly Hogan, inventor of the Painter's Pal. Courtesy of Susan Casey.

Creators Program, a national program sponsored by the U.S. Patent and Trademark Office and other organizations that is open to all students in grades seven through twelve. She was the national winner in the household inventions category in 1995 for her invention. She called it the "Painter's Pal."

Molly thought of the idea for her invention one day when she was painting on the lawn outside her home. Her mother called out to her that she had a phone call. When Molly started to put the paint brush down on the lawn her mother called, "No, don't put it there." So Molly started to put the brush on the top of the paint can. Her mom called, "No, don't put it there." Then Molly started to put it on a sheet of newspaper. Again her mom called, "No, don't put it there." Molly thought, "Where can I put it?" That was her problem. So when her class assignment was to think of an invention, she invented a device that hangs on the side of a paint can. It holds the brush so that the paint drips into a container.

Other students enter the Young Inventors and Creators Program as individuals. How? They fill out an entry form and ask the principal of the school to sign it. It isn't necessary for them to have participated in a program at the school. All that matters is that they have a model of an invention. That was the case with Robin Lawson. She designed a new type of snowboard. She loved the sport, but after she fell down repeatedly trying to get onto the ski lift with her snowboard, she thought there ought to be a change in design. So she created a device that was attached to the board and allowed her foot to swivel so that it was easier to get on the lift. She has since worked with her father and applied for a patent. To enter the Young Inventors and Creators Program she got the signature of her school principal and submitted her invention as an individual entry. She was one of the national winners in 1995.

Companies also sponsor invention contests. Duracell is one such company. Duracell USA is administered by the National Science

Robin Lawson with her Snowboard. Courtesy of Robin Lawson.

Teachers Association and challenges students in grades nine through twelve to create devices powered by Duracell batteries.

Like what? Laurie DiStefano invented the Turn Signal Turner Offer in 1989. She was then a senior at St. Mark's High School in Wilmington, Delaware. "My father would always turn his turn signal on when he was changing lanes, and we'd end up driving with it on for hours," Laurie explained. She was tired of that. So she invented a device that automatically turns the turn signal off after two minutes.

What's Laurie's advice to other student inventors? "My teacher was a tough grader. Our whole class did inventions for the competition, and very few people got As. Mine didn't do particularly well. I got maybe a B- or C. So I just want people to know that not everybody might fall in love with your idea, but I think it's important to have confidence in yourself and to pursue what you want to do."

Trisha Buss, inventor of the Rub-Yer-Back Suntan Oil Dispenser.
Courtesy of Janet Buss.

Silver Burdett & Ginn is a textbook publishing company that sponsors the annual Invention Convention for students, kindergarten through twelfth grade, in schools that use their science books. Participants follow the same process inventors do in applying for a patent.

Trisha Buss, age nine, of Plainview, Nebraska, was the 1995 winner in the primary division with her Rub-Yer-Back Suntan Oil Dispenser. Trisha connected a squeeze bottle full of suntan oil with a piece of aquarium tubing to a back scratcher covered with a sponge mitt for applying the oil. It was just the invention for the beach.

INVENTORS CLUB OF AMERICA honors students for new products. Sisters Jeanie and Elizabeth Low of Houston, Texas, ages thirteen and ten, both patent holders, were honored by the club in 1996. Jeanie invented the Kiddie Stool to make it easy for children to reach the bathroom sink. Elizabeth invented a shapable surgical glove paperweight and a "fire-aware" mattress cover. "There are problems and you try to solve them," said Jeannie.

If students are finalists in any of the nationwide invention or problem-solving programs or competitions, or if their invention is being manufactured or patented, they are eligible to submit their names to be considered for the National Gallery for America's Young Inventors. The gallery was established in 1996 to celebrate the inventiveness of America's youth. Each year six young inventors in kindergarten through twelfth grade from across the country are honored. The display of the work of young inventors is in the same building as the National Inventors Hall of Fame. The first young inventors were inducted in 1996, and three of the six were young women: Kara Levine, Alexia Abernathy, and the team of Elizabeth Nathan and Gabriella Pollack.

Kara Levine of New York developed Karink, an environmentally friendly newspaper printing ink. This ink, which "uses a solvent derived from pine trees, results in a newspaper ink with low volatility . . . (which) reduces air pollution." Kara was attending high school in Panama City, Florida, when she invented it. She produced five hundred pounds of the ink that was used to print an entire edition of the *Panama City News Herald*. Properties of the ink may allow newspapers to use lighter weight paper, thus potentially reducing costs. Kara went on to attend New York University. She wants to combine her art and chemistry interests to pursue a career as an art restorer.

Alexia Abernathy, a tenth-grader in 1996, invented the Oops! Proof No-Spill Feeding Bowl when she was eleven. She participated then in Invent, Iowa!, a statewide invention program. When she had to come up with an idea for an invention, she thought about the problems of her baby-sitter's two-year-old son, Charles. "He couldn't walk and eat at the same time. His food kept spilling out of his bowl," said Alexia. So Alexia made a special bowl for him. She put a small bowl holding his food inside a larger bowl, then attached a lid to the larger bowl. The trick was that she cut a large hole in the lid. The lid kept the small bowl from falling out, but Charles could reach in the hole to get his food. If he tipped the bowl, the food would spill into the larger bowl rather than onto the floor. "The bowl is designed to be completely spill-proof at the time when children are learning to feed themselves and increase their independence," said Alexia.

After Alexia entered the contest, she and her dad thought the invention might make a good product. They checked in stores to make sure a product like hers did not exist, then Alexia wrote letters

Oops! Proof No-Spill Feeding Bowl. Courtesy Little Kids, Inc.

to companies asking if they wanted to make her product. Her letter began with the sentences: "I'm Alexia. I'm a fifth-grader, and I'm an inventor." While some companies were not interested, Little Kids was. Alexia, her dad, and the company Little Kids secured a patent for her bowl, which is now manufactured by them and sold in stores nationwide.

Elizabeth Nathan and Gabriella Pollack, a team, both attended The Brearly School in New York City. When they heard about the 1995 NYNEX Science and Technology Awards Competition, Elizabeth told Gabriella, "It would be a good way to spend more time together." So they entered. They invented a nonreusable syringe out of concern about the spread of the AIDS virus via the sharing of needles. Because one of their family members suffered from a medical condition requiring injections, the girls had access to used syringes. They started working with the syringes and created and discarded fourteen different designs before arriving at their final design. What did they come up with? A mechanism inside the barrel of the syringe locks in place after one use. Elizabeth and Gabriella won first place in the contest. That win garnered them a summer project working on further development of their idea with engineering and business professors at Columbia University.

"We are exploring the manufacturability and marketability of our design with the engineering and business professors. We visited an injection molding company, and we are talking to mechanical engineers about materials we might use for production of our syringe. We are learning not only about engineering but about how to take an idea from paper to market. We both feel very lucky," said Elizabeth. Both young women entered Harvard in the fall of 1996.

When students create inventions for programs or contests, all the other students in their class or school can see their accomplishments. Students can learn from each other. Contests are a way for young people to try out their inventing skills. And when women inventors receive awards, the world discovers their accomplishments.

5 *Women Gain Patents*

"When you believe in an idea, there is a way of succeeding. Never be afraid of jumping in. That's what life is, a series of problems to be solved."
— *Rebecca Schroeder, inventor, Glo Sheet*

Sybilla Masters of Philadelphia, Pennsylvania, was a busy woman. Everyone knew that. She was wife to Thomas Masters, a prosperous Quaker merchant who was mayor of Philadelphia in the early 1700s. While she raised their four children, she tinkered. She had a talent for mechanical invention and an interest in the way people around her did their work. She watched the Tuscadora Indians grind corn by hand. They put it in a mortar, a stone bowl, and stamped it with a stone pestle. That was interesting to Sybilla. In her day, most corn was turned into meal by a grinding process, with power from waterwheels. After considering this, Sybilla thought of another way. She created a device for stamping the corn based on the mortar and pestle that could be powered by horses or waterwheels. That meant the mills could be located near the corn fields, not just near rivers, the power source for waterwheels. Her device also included trays for cleaning and setting the corn out to dry.

She wanted to get a patent to protect her new invention. Because Pennsylvania was then one of the English colonies, she needed to get an English patent.

Sybilla stood up at a meeting of her Quaker congregation and told them of her plans. She would be traveling to London to secure a patent for her invention. In 1715 English Patent Number 401 was granted to Thomas Masters for his wife Sybilla's invention of a device for "cleaning and curing the Indian corn growing in several colonies in America." That was the first time a woman living in what was to become the United States was acknowledged for an invention with a patent, even though it was not in her name. Then the property of married women was owned by their husbands. And patents were property. She later sold the corn milled with her device through her husband's company. She called her product Tuscadora Rice.

Seventy-five years later, on April 10, 1790, fourteen years after America became an independent nation, President George Washington signed the bill that made it possible for inventors to obtain patents in the United States. In 1809, Mrs. Mary Kies, a hat-maker from Connecticut, was the first woman in the United States to receive a patent in her own name. Hats were then popular with New England women. Mary's patent was for a way of making hats using "a method to weave straw with silk and thread." Having a patent allowed her to make and sell hats made with her method while preventing others from using that same method in hatmaking. First Lady Dolley Madison, wife of President James Madison, heard of Mary's achievements and sent congratulations.

Mary Kies wanted a patent because patents were created to protect people who are in business. A patent gives the inventor, and only the inventor, the right to prevent others from making, using, and selling an invention for a period of time. Not every idea for a product can be an invention. An invention of a machine, design, plant, or process has to be new. It cannot be something that has been invented before, but it can be an innovation, an improvement of an existing invention.

An invention also has to be useful—something that others can use, something of value. It also has to be unobvious—something that wouldn't just naturally occur to anyone who is knowledgeable in the field of the invention.

Many other women have followed Mary Kies's lead in gaining patents for their inventions. In 1843 Nancy Johnson invented the ice-cream freezer. Other women gained patents for keeping bees, storing eggs, and keeping chickens. Mary Jane Montgomery gained a patent in 1864 for devising a way to improve locomotive wheels. In the 1870s Sarah Ruth noticed that horses do not have any protection from the sun. Men and women had hats. Why not horses? She applied for and gained a patent in 1873 for her Sunshade for Horses.

Other women gained patents for engines and stoves. Louisa Simpson's 1878 patent was for destroying vegetation on railways. In 1885 Sarah Goode of Chicago, an African American, gained a patent for an office desk that folded out to become a bed. Desk by day. Bed by night. Her goal was to save space. In 1918 Minnie Blau invented a device for teaching arithmetic. Merry Hull, whose real name was Gladys Whitcomb Geissman, was an industrial designer in New York in the 1930s and one of four winners of a $1,000 prize from Lord & Taylor, a New York department store, for her new design of a commercial product—gloves. In the 1970s Barbara Askins, working at NASA, was granted a patent for a way of creating clearer photographs of space. In 1985 Gabrielle Knecht, a successful clothing designer from New York, won the prestigious More Fashion Award for her clothing designed for movement. "Clothing does not show that we can hug ourselves from the front and not from the back," said Gabrielle, "so I thought, 'what if we fit clothing to the way we move?'" She gained a patent in 1984 for the angle of the sleeve direction in relation to the body—a first in the world of fashion. The Gabrielle Knecht label is sold at Saks Fifth Avenue and other stores.

In the 1990s Janine Jagger, an associate professor of neurosurgery at the University of Virginia Health Sciences Center, and a team of her colleagues received patents for six safety needle devices that prevent needlestick injuries in health care.

Each of the women inventors had to first determine whether her idea for an invention was, in fact, a new one. Because an invention must be new, inventors cannot receive a patent if someone else has already patented their idea. How do inventors know? They do a patent search. Many inventors do their own patent searches at the U.S. Patent and Trademark Office in Arlington, Virginia, or at one of seventy-eight Patent Deposit Libraries around the United States. At any of those places inventors can read about any of more than five million patents that have been granted. Luckily, inventors doing a patent search have to read only about patents that have been granted for similar inventions.

Is it difficult? Not really. But doing a patent search is time-consuming. Just ask teacher Pat Bradel whose sixth-grade class at Simmons Elementary School in Clayton, New Jersey, conducted one. After they created their version of the perfect ice-cream cone, they wanted to know if the design was original. They researched the history of the ice-cream cone and made two hundred attempts at creating a cone before they were satisfied with their creation of a whole wheat, dripless cone.

When they started on the patent search, they were in for more research. "When you do a search you can't just look at items exactly like yours; you have to look in related areas as well," said Pat. "Since the cone was made of waffles, they had to look at the patents for waffles and other areas you wouldn't even think of. They only did a partial search, but that required a review of over one-hundred patents. They did it all by hand since the material was not on computer. It was fun but tedious." For their efforts, Pat's students — Megan Keys, Gillian Keys, Douglas Bastow, Daniel Dantinne, and Song Yang Heil — won the 1990 Invention and Problem Solving Competition of Cognetics, a national problem solving program.

Filling out a patent application is another challenge. Because patent applications can be complicated, many inventors hire a patent attorney or a patent agent either to help them with their application or to review their applications after they have filled them out. Applying for and maintaining a patent costs thousands of dollars.

In 1966 Andrea and John Tierney of Stockton, California, wanted to obtain a patent for The Bug House, a screened container for holding live bugs. It all started when Andrea's daughters collected some live bugs and wanted her to hold them. Andrea didn't like holding live bugs. Because she was an artist, with many different materials on hand, she found a piece of screen, rolled it up, attached a lid to one end, put the bugs in it, and then attached a lid to the other end. It was as if she created a jar, not of glass but of screen. Her daughters immediately used it to look at their bugs. The neighbor's kids wanted one for themselves. Andrea showed it to her husband, also an artist, and they discussed the possibility of making the screen cages as a product for kids. Together they designed and created a more sophisticated design of The Bug House. It looked almost like a Chinese lantern. It has the same design today.

Andrea and John began manufacturing The Bug House in their own house and sold their first products in a local store. Once they began selling it, they had only one year from the date of the first sale in which to file a U.S. patent application. That is the patent law. Inventors must file within one year of selling or otherwise making their invention known to the public if they wish to receive a valid patent. They announce inventions by entering contests or by talking about them at conferences or writing about them in magazines or journals. If they file after more than a year, they cannot receive a valid patent.

When Andrea and John filled out their patent application with the U.S. Patent and Trademark Office, they had to explain why their bug holder was better than what already existed. So they wrote:

Andrea Tierney, coinventor of The Bug House. Courtesy of John Tierney.

"Often children use a tin can or cardboard box to save insects . . . [but] it is difficult to observe the insects. . . . Children will often use a glass jar [but] it can be highly dangerous [if] dropped and shattered into jagged pieces of broken glass. . . ." Then they explained why The Bug House was better: "It affords ready ventilation for the creatures, enables easy observation . . . and is completely safe to use by small children . . . and the device is virtually unbreakable."

After being granted Patent Number 3,272,376, Andrea and John also registered a trademark for the name and design of the words "The Bug House." Although Andrea died several years ago, John and their daughters continue to manufacture the bug holder. The profits from its sales have paid for the college educations of the girls who had collected those first bugs.

PATENTS LAST FOR a period of only fourteen to twenty years from their filing date. They are designed to protect inventors as they begin a business; during that time, if inventors discover that someone is making and selling a product based on their invention, they have the legal right to make them stop. Or they can demand that the other company pay for the right to use their invention.

After a patent has expired, an invention becomes part of the public domain. That means that the invention can be made and sold by anyone. To keep the patent protection, inventors often create an improvement on their invention — an innovation — and gain another patent and continued protection.

Not every inventor applies for a patent. Bette Graham didn't. She was the inventor of Liquid Paper. At the time she created the quick-drying paint, she could not afford the costs of applying. She protected her invention in another way — by using a trademark. A trademark is either a word, phrase, symbol, or design that identifies a product. She trademarked the name Liquid Paper.

Applying for and gaining a trademark can cost less than $500 — less expensive than applying for a patent. Another advantage is that, unlike a patent, a trademark does not expire. It must be renewed, but it lasts indefinitely. Some other famous trademarks are Kleenex, Xerox, and Levi's. A capital R in a circle (®)next to an image or name indicates the name is trademarked for the entire United States. "TM" is another symbol for a trademark.

Cost is not the only reason inventors gain a trademark instead of a patent. To apply for a patent, an inventor must reveal the way a product is made and its ingredients. That's why the owners of Coca-Cola did not gain a patent. They did not want to reveal the secret ingredient in the drink that makes the taste so unusual. The recipe for Coca-Cola is a trade secret.

Not all trademarks are the same. Think of the way the words "Liquid Paper" or "Coca-Cola" appear on the containers. Those images are trademarked. As with a patent, if another company uses the same name or image, the company with the trademark can take legal action to stop them.

When Dran Reese of Monrovia, California, created QuakeHold, a putty-like substance that can be placed under objects to secure them to tabletops or shelves, she did not want to reveal the ingredients. "If we patented it we would have to reveal the chemical composition. Then anyone could have made it," said Dran. She filed instead for trademark protection. If others make a copycat product, her attorney writes a letter demanding that they stop making a product that looks like QuakeHold. Who uses her product? Thousands of people in Los Angeles and Japan have used it to secure their glassware to shelves and tables during earthquakes of the last few years.

Trademarks protect designs and images as well. The trademark is not only for the words "Liquid Paper" or "Coca-Cola" but also for the design of the bottles and the cans. Trademarks are also granted for building designs. McDonald's has a trademark for the design of the buildings with the familiar golden arches.

Many inventors file applications for both a patent and registration of a trademark. After the patent expires, a trademark continues to protect their product. Customers recognize the product because of its trademarked name and package design.

Trademarks and patents have been granted to many women inventors since 1809. From then until the 1970s, even though many women were inventing, women gained only 1.5 percent of all U.S. patents. Why? Many women filed for patents in the name of their husbands. Others filed under the names of men who provided or raised the money to manufacture their inventions. In those cases, the women's names do not appear in the patent records.

Since the 1970s the number of patents granted to women has risen steadily. In 1983 the percentage of patents with women listed as an inventor was 3.5 percent. In 1996, the percentage had risen to 9.25

percent. The rising number reflects the growing number of women being hired as engineers and scientists. It also reflects the increase in the number of independent women inventors, ones who have created inventions and started businesses to sell their patented products.

Not all patents are the same. When inventors apply for a patent, they have to choose to apply for one of three types of patents: a utility patent, a design patent, or a plant patent.

Margaret Knight gained a utility patent for her Paper Bag Folding Machine. Patsy Sherman gained a utility patent for Scotchgard. So did Lydia O'Leary when she gained one for Covermark. Most patents are utility patents. They are granted for a machine with moving parts or for items like paper or hair clips that don't have moving parts. They are granted for a new process, like for the steps in creating a drug for medical use, or for creating a new composition of matter, like a new salad dressing, shampoo, fertilizer, or peanut butter.

Design patents are granted for appearance—for any new, original, and ornamental design for a product. If one is granted for a clock that looks like a spaceship, the patent is not granted for how the clock works but for the way the clock looks. Design patents are granted for designs of chairs, cars, clothes, phones, bicycles, teapots, baby carriers, and many more items.

When Ruane Jeter created a new design for the household toaster, she didn't apply for a utility patent; she applied for and received a design patent. Why? Her patent was not for how the toaster worked but for how it looked. During the 1980s Ruane was studying industrial design at California State University at Los Angeles. She was thinking about creating a new design for an ordinary item when she realized the toaster had not been redesigned in some time.

So she started drawing sketches until she came up with her final design, which she called "The Tiltster" because it tilts toward the user. Its shape is like the letter V lying on its side. A person standing in front of it can look right into the area where the bread is placed.

Ruane's design makes it much easier for young children or those with disabilities to insert bread, waffles, or tarts for toasting. She gained patents in both the United States and the United Kingdom and was honored as a modern African American inventor.

How about a design patent for a diaper? That's what Harriet Clough of Meadville, Pennsylvania, gained in 1959. Her diaper was a design suited to would-be baby sheriffs. Because she didn't have to worry about how the diaper worked, only how it looked, her patent shows a drawing of a diaper with holsters on the sides and a sheriff's badge on the front.

Ecologist Georgia A. Bost of Houston didn't apply for a utility or a design patent when she bred a new type of hibiscus plant. Inventors who create distinct and new varieties of apples, daisies, strawberries, plums, geraniums, roses, or other plants are granted plant patents. Georgia gained one in 1995 for a hibiscus plant that she named "Quatro Rojo." She bred a new variety by crossing three native plants of the United States and a commercial variety bred from different U.S. plants by the Japanese. "I'm not just breeding for the flower but to create a very vigorous, productive plant, one that grows rapidly and big. Quatro Rojo will grow 12 to 15 feet in one year." Most other hibiscus of this type grow to be only 4 to 5 feet tall. That's why Georgia's hibiscus plant can receive a patent. It is new. It is different from existing hibiscus plants. How does she breed a new variety? She takes the pollen from an existing variety and places it on the stigma of another variety. Once that pollenates and makes seeds, she takes the seeds—hundreds of them—plants them, and watches as they grow. She looks for a plant that is different from the others, as was Quatro Rojo.

When she began testing, developing, and patenting new hybrids of hibiscus from different existing species of North America, Georgia's goal was to create a hardy plant that could be made into different products. The hardy stems of Quatro Rojo can be used for making

Quatro Rojo. Courtesy of Georgia Best.

fabric or fiberboard. The plants themselves can be used for land-
scaping. The flowers can be used as food. "They are delicious in

salads, as a vinegar, or for tea," claimed Georgia, who works as an ecologist doing environmental consulting and land studies for companies in Texas. She also registered the trademark "Bost" for her products.

NOT EVERYONE WHO applies for a patent is granted one. In the l980s Mildred Smith of Washington, D.C., who performed with the National Negro Opera Company, had her patent application turned down. Her application was for a card game about family relationships. She called the game "Family Treeditions." The name of her game combines the idea of a family tree and the traditions attached to families. Each card has a designation — mother, father, brother, up to fourth cousin — and each is worth points ranging from one to ten. When people played the game, they could figure out how people in a family are related to each other.

After Mildred sent her application in to the U.S. Patent and Trademark Office, the patent examiner read the application and did research to see if her idea for the invention was new and useful. Mildred's patent examiner turned down her application because he said there was another game like it.

Mildred didn't want to be turned down. Her invention was important to her. She had gotten the idea for her invention while she was suffering from the effects of multiple sclerosis and couldn't move for a period of time. While recovering in bed, she started thinking about her family, about her mother, her cousins, her aunts, and her uncles. What was their relationship to each other? She wondered. When she could move again, she completed her game that made it easy for family members to figure out their relationships to each other.

As part of the patent process, Mildred could talk to the patent examiner who turned down her application. She went to his office and spent a couple of hours describing the game to him. "When I was finished, he said, 'I see now.' He understood. It passed the test. I got my patent," said Mildred.

After printing up five thousand decks of her cards, Mildred sold the game by playing it with family members at reunions, at sororities and fraternities, and at senior centers. "I sat down with two little boys from church and showed them how to play," said Mildred. "They knew of their aunt, their mother or father but they didn't know how to put together the relationships. 'Your mother has a sister, doesn't she?' I said to them. 'What is she to you?' 'That's my . . . that's my. . . .' They kept hem-hawing and see-sawing. They had not thought about their aunt being their mother's sister. Or their father's brother being their uncle.

"Even some of the seniors didn't know some of their kin. Some of them knew nothing about making connections with first, second, third, or fourth cousins. The game opens up a line of thought. So that's how I sell the games.

"Family relationships are very important," said Mildred. "So many things can develop from that." She was granted Patent Number 4,230,321 for her card game and later honored during Black History Month as a Black Inventor. Mildred died in 1993 when she was seventy-eight years old.

Another inventor, Anne Macdonald, made three attempts to gain a patent for Great Scott Argyler, a machine that makes it easier to knit multicolored strands of yarn without tangling. Even though she hired attorneys on the first two tries, the description of her machine did not seem original to patent examiners. But Anne did not think the lawyers had explained it correctly. "That still isn't the way," she told her second lawyer. Finally she went before the patent examiners herself. Her explanation convinced them. She was granted her patent in 1984.

Many others have not been as fortunate as Mildred and Anne. Many of those who have applied for patents have been turned down. Sometimes it is because the inventions are not new, useful, or unobvious. In 1995 more than 210,000 patent applications were filed, and more than 100,000 patents were granted.

Many young women are being granted patents. In 1971 ten-year-old Rebecca Schroeder was the youngest person to have ever received a U.S. patent. Her efforts started quite simply. She wanted to be able to write in the dark. One day, while her mother was shopping, Rebecca waited in the car and did her math homework. When the sun started to set, she didn't have enough light.

While in the car Rebecca thought there should be a way for her to do her homework in the dark. She remembered seeing phosphorescent paint at the hardware store. If you shine a light on phosphorescent paint, it glows for a period of time after the light is removed. After a trip to the hardware store with her father, Rebecca painted a piece of cardboard with the phosphorescent paint and waited for it to dry. She then exposed it to ordinary light and placed several sheets of paper over it and went into the darkest room in the house—the bathroom. Light shone through the paper. She could write on the paper—in the dark. "It works, it works!" she shouted to her parents as she ran into the playroom.

"She was born into the right family," said her father, Charles Schroeder, who happens to be a patent attorney, the type of lawyer who helps inventors apply for patents. He thought Rebecca had a good idea. He helped her file an application for a patent. She called it a "Glo Sheet" and received her first patent in 1973.

At first Rebecca didn't understand what it meant to have a patent, but her father reassured her: "It's a good thing to have your name on an idea." That is one value of a patent. It is a way of telling the world of one's ideas.

A patent has another importance. It is a way of protecting ideas of people who want to sell the products made from their inventions. In

Rebecca Schroeder using her invention, the Glo Sheet. Courtesy of Herral Long.

Rebecca's case, she received ten patents—her original patent and nine additional patents she was granted for improvements on her original Glo Sheet. The patents all help protect her invention as her property. The Glo Sheet was soon used by nurses on night duty in hospitals as they made their rounds to patients' rooms. Now they didn't have to wake patients by turning on the lights. U.S. Navy personnel used her Glo Sheet when working at night on the decks of ships. Rebecca also developed a battery-operated version called the Glo Panel. She sells her products through her own company, B. J. Products, in Toledo, Ohio.

Today, women and girl inventors are more active than they have ever been before in history. Girls are actively entering many local, state, and nationwide contests for inventors. Women and girl inventors are continuing to apply for and be granted patents and trademarks. They are carrying on the tradition started by early inventors in creating inventions and products that make their lives easier and that benefit the world.

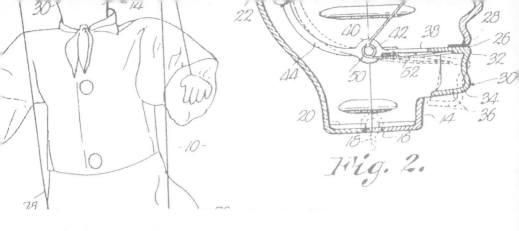

Fig. 2.

6 | *From Model to Product*

"I think anyone who is making progress faces fear. You have to overcome fear. Overcoming fear is all there is to success. You have to face fears and doubts constantly. You keep doing it over and over."

— *Bette Graham, inventor, Liquid Paper*

ette Nesmith Graham made a mistake on a freelance art project and painted right over it. That's how she got the idea. Why not paint over my mistakes at the office? "An artist never corrects by erasing," she once said, "but always paints over the error."

Why was that important? Bette was an executive secretary at Texas Bank & Trust. It was difficult to erase typing mistakes. Retyping her work took a lot of time. Bette wanted to do well at her job. She was in her twenties and divorced from her husband. She needed to support herself and her young son.

So Bette decided to take her paint brush and paint to the office and just cover her mistakes. For several years she kept it a secret. Then others began to notice. One boss told her not to put that "white stuff" on his letters. But the other secretaries wanted some of their own.

Bette Graham with her invention, Liquid Paper. Courtesy of The Gillette Company.

Bette sold her first bottles of Mistake Out, the first name she gave her product, in 1956.

As Bette used and sold her product she worked on developing a better paint — one that dried quickly and matched the color of paper used by most offices. She researched formulas for paint at the library, talked to those knowledgeable about paint, and ground and mixed her own paint by hand in her kitchen laboratory. That was the beginning of what was later named Liquid Paper, the correction fluid used by students, office workers, artists, architects, and anyone else who wants to cover a mistake.

Bette's kitchen became her manufacturing plant. Manufacturing includes all the steps of making a product by hand or machine. At that time Bette made and mixed batches of her paint by hand. Then she and her son, Michael Nesmith (who would later become a member of the musical group, The Monkees), poured it into small bottles, trimmed paint brushes, and attached labels, all by hand. Later Michael and his friends did the work. Those were the steps involved in manufacturing.

By 1957 Bette was selling several hundred bottles a month while she continued working as a secretary. Because she was not able to afford the fees to obtain a patent, she gained a trademark for the name of her product. Anyone seeing it would know it was hers. When she also began selling Mistake Out to local office supply stores, her sales increased. Then she contacted magazines like *The Office* and *The Secretary* that were read by office workers and supply stores. When articles appeared, Bette received orders from across the country.

Once she was able to support herself from the sales of Mistake Out, Bette traveled to sell it to stores throughout Texas. In 1962 she married Robert Graham, who was experienced in sales. Together they sold Mistake Out throughout the southern and western United States.

By 1968, when the product name was changed to Liquid Paper, the company had grossed more than $1 million. By 1975 the company employed two hundred people, and in 1976 it produced twenty-five million bottles. In 1979 Bette sold her company to the Gillette Corporation for $47.5 million.

Bette decided to use her money to help others, especially women. She established several foundations that award grants to women in business and the arts. When she died in 1980, she left half her fortune to her son and half to her foundations.

Today Liquid Paper is manufactured in a factory. The paint is mixed in large quantities in vats. Paint is poured into the bottles by a machine. Labels are affixed by other machines. Everything that Bette and Michael did by hand is now done by a machine. Whether done by hand or machine, the process is still called manufacturing.

MANUFACTURING CAN TAKE place in a home, office, factory, or field. Where manufacturing takes place depends on what is involved in making the product. Can the product be made at home? Can it be manufactured in an office or warehouse? Does it need to be made in a scientific laboratory? On a farm or in a creamery? Does a mold need to be created for a part of a toy or a doll?

How a product is made or manufactured depends on the product as well. The process of manufacturing Liquid Paper would have to be different from the process of making clothing, cars, tables, machinery, puppets, Scotchgard, or frozen pizza.

Yes, even frozen pizza and other foods can be inventions. Rose Totino, the first woman elected to the Frozen Food Hall of Fame, was granted a patent for her frozen pizza crust in 1977. And when she began to manufacture frozen pizzas, the process was very different from the manufacturing process of Liquid Paper.

Rose came from a poor family. Her parents moved to the United States from Italy in 1910. Because she and her family often went to bed hungry, Rose was forced to quit school at age sixteen to help pay expenses. She did housework for $2.50 an hour at homes near their own in Minneapolis, Minnesota.

Rose's mother loved to cook pizza the way they do in Italy. Rose made pizza, too, as she was growing up. After she married Jim Totino, a baker, she continued to make pizza, and as their children started school, Rose became active in the PTA and often made pizzas for the meetings. That was in the 1940s. Then most people outside of New York or Los Angeles had never heard of pizza. But once they tasted Rose's pizzas they started asking her to make ones for them.

As they had more and more requests for pizzas, Rose and Jim thought about opening a take-out pizza restaurant. That was in 1951. But they needed money—$1,500. That's when they decided to go to the bank to apply for a loan.

Rose was a natural salesperson. She knew how to interest people in her product. When she and Jim went before the loan committee, along with presenting their business plan, Rose served pizza. She

Rose Totino with her patented Totino's Frozen Pizza. Courtesy of the Pillsbury Company.

brought along a portable oven and cooked the pizza at the bank. She wanted the committee members to know what they were investing in. After they tasted the pizza, the committee gave the Totinos the loan.

After their restaurant was open for more than ten years, Rose and Jim decided to try to sell frozen pizza. At that time only one company in America was selling frozen pizza. Rose and Jim wanted to make a better one using her mother's recipe of tomato sauce and herbs. They also wanted to add Italian sausage and mozzarella cheese to the recipe.

To be successful, they had to figure out a way to quickly make lots of frozen pizzas. Then Jim got an idea. Why not put the frozen pizza crusts on the turntable of his record player? It was an old one that worked with a foot peddle. Press the foot pedal and the turntable would go around. They put the frozen pizzas on the turntable as if they were records. As the crust went around, the Totinos squirted sauce on it through a plastic tube. It took no time at all. That made it easy to prepare a lot of pizzas in a short time. There was only one problem: the foot pedal gave them an electric shock. They got a lot of shocks making those first frozen pizzas. That was the way they manufactured the pizzas.

Totino's Finer Foods became a nationwide business. Rose hired brokers, people who will sell a product in different towns, to sell her pizzas across the country. She relied on her common sense to hire people she thought would do a good job for her. To reward her brokers she treated them to trips to Italy. Rose's original goal was to make a living and to have fun. And she did.

Totino's frozen pizzas are available today in markets across the United States. In 1975 the Pillsbury Company purchased the Totinos's pizza business for $20 million. Rose gained a patent for her pizza crust based on her mother's recipe and became the first female vice president in the history of the Pillsbury Company.

Manufacturing frozen pizzas required a very different process from the one used in manufacturing Liquid Paper. Manufacturing the pizzas required lots of testing to see if the crust was just right. Did it taste like Rose's mom's crust even after it was frozen and reheated? What about the sauce? How did it taste? Those things mattered in the manufacturing of frozen pizza. And today what Rose and Jim did by hand is now done in a factory, mainly by machines.

Manufacturing is different depending on the product. No one cares how Liquid Paper tastes. No one eats it. People do care about its color and about how quickly it dries. How a product is manufactured depends entirely on what is important about the product. What are the materials? How strong or fragile does it need to be? Who will use it? All of those questions need to be answered in deciding how best to manufacture a product.

HAZELLE ROLLINS FACED completely different manufacturing problems than Bette and Rose when she wanted to make her product: a stringed puppet, a marionette. That was in 1929. She was then an art student at the University of Kansas. When a neighbor boy received a marionette from Italy, he asked Hazelle to make him another one. Hazelle studied the Italian puppet and constructed one of her own. To make the head she carved it by hand out of wood. She handpainted the face. Soon Hazelle was creating lots of marionettes for herself and for others, writing plays for them, and putting on shows for school kids.

In what way was Hazelle an inventor? A puppet show is always more fun if the puppets move like humans. Can they bend, move their legs, open their mouths? Hazelle began experimenting with ways to make them move. She gained four patents for her "airplane controls," methods of moving the puppets. Hazelle's controls made it easier to move the puppets and to keep the strings from being tangled. Even children could manipulate them easily. "Children become experts!" read one of her advertisements. "A twist of the wrist and

Hazelle Rollins. Courtesy of the Puppetry Guild.

they dance into life, for Hazelle's Marionettes are easy to operate," read another.

Children could choose from more than two hundred different characters offered by Hazelle, Inc., the company Hazelle founded to manufacture not only her stringed puppets but also hand and finger puppets. Animal characters included ducks, rabbits, lions, and birds. Marionettes included Bo-Peep, Boy Blue, Hillbilly Man, Soldier, Nurse, Clown, Uncle Sam, Fortune Teller, and the most popular character, Teto the Clown, who wore a red polka-dot suit.

Hazelle began manufacturing marionettes in the recreation room of her home. She sold her first puppets to stores in Kansas City. As she began selling more, she rented a factory. By 1933 she had enough orders to found a company — Hazelle, Inc. When Hazelle married J. Woodson Rollins, an industrial engineer, just before World War II, he was working in an airplane factory. He applied his knowledge of the assembly line to puppet construction. By 1947 Hazelle had more than fifty employees, and her company was producing one thousand puppets a week. It became the largest puppet company in the United States. By 1971 two hundred and fifty thousand hand, finger, and string puppets a year were being manufactured by Hazelle, Inc. They were sold all over the world.

While Hazelle was running her company, she also continued as a puppeteer. When she was asked to stage puppet shows she often enlisted her daughter Nancy and her son John as fellow puppeteers. How were the fragile marionettes manufactured? Hazelle's daughter Nancy remembers visiting the factory and seeing how the puppets were made. While Hazelle carved the first heads by hand out of wood and hired a shoemaker to carve the first shoes and hands,

HAZELLE'S *Little Play* THEATRE

presents

"Spring Fever"

(A one-act Playlet for Marionettes)

CHARACTERS

PENNIE, a pretty, brunette school girl.

ROBINHOOD, dashing performer from the Circus near Pennie's home.

TETO, the bragging, playful Clown, also from the Circus.

Use "Outdoor" scenery backdrop furnished with your new stage. The playlet opens with PENNIE in her back yard, sitting on a bench. Music is heard in the background. It is Spring!

PENNIE *(Humming part of a song).* Oh, dear, I wish I didn't have to go back to school this afternoon. *(Sighs.)* I guess I must have Spring Fever! *(Gets up and walks to side of stage as if looking at something on the ground. Aloud, she speaks to herself).* But if I don't go to school I won't make good grades and be on the honor roll.

NEW MARIONETTE THEATRE

Big, durable Freezurboard stage in four colors, folds compactly when not in use. It is 31" high, 39" wide, and 18" deep. Changeable indoor and outdoor scenery backdrops are furnished. Plan your own "shows" with this stage. (Not Mailable—Available at your local stores or shipped via Express or Freight.)

ROBINHOOD *(Entering from left of stage. He has been watching PENNIE).* Aw, shucks, one afternoon wouldn't make any difference in your grades, would it?

PENNIE *(Jumps back away from him).* Oh! Who are you? Go away, I wasn't talking to you or anyone else.

ROBINHOOD. It's a wonderful day, isn't it. Just too nice to be inside. Hear that robin? *(Sings).* When the Red-Red Robin goes Bob-Bob-Bobbing along.

(Continued on other side)

Hazelle's Little Play Theatre playlet "Spring Fever"

Nancy recalled that later ones were made of a plastic material called tenite. Molds were created so that many could be made at once. "The tenite came in the form of plastic pellets," said Nancy. "Fifty-gallon drums of it were poured into the molds, then heated and the plastic was forced in. It got quite hot. A man wearing asbestos gloves would remove the heads and other pieces from the molds.

"The factory consisted of all sorts of work stations. There was a spray booth. Different masks were placed over the heads so that the features of the face could be painted. Then parts of the face like the freckles and the eyes were handpainted. Another area was full of sewing machines and the ladies made the costumes." Costumes included the gown for Princess Cinderella, the patch jeans for the Strawman, the wings for the Blue Fairy, and Teto's red polka-dot suit.

"Another area was a stringing booth," said Nancy. "There were horizontal poles. The controls were on the top and the puppets would be placed so that their feet touched the table. Then the person in the booth would tie the strings to the hands and feet of the puppets." Otherwise the puppets wouldn't move correctly.

So even though the manufacturing of a fragile item like a marionette was done in a factory, many parts of it were done by hand. It was not the type of product that could be made entirely by machines.

Hazelle, who founded the Puppeteers of America, added one other element to the manufacturing process. She wrote playlets to go with each puppet. The idea was that the children receiving the puppet could then easily stage their own shows.

Hazelle was named one of the Outstanding Business Women of the Year in Missouri in 1969. She operated her company until 1975 and died in 1984 when she was seventy-four.

Paint, pizza, and puppets are each manufactured in a different way. Manufacturing is different depending on what is involved in making the product.

NOT EVERY INVENTOR wants to or can make a product at home. Many inventors want to think of an idea, make a model or prototype of it, and then license or sell it to a company. How? Inventors present their models to companies that manufacture and sell products. If a company is interested, the inventor can sell it outright. That means the company pays the inventor a certain amount of money. Then the company owns the invention. The inventor gives up all further rights to the invention. If the company makes or loses money it does not affect the inventor. That's what happens when an inventor sells an invention.

Inventors can also license their inventions to companies. A license usually lasts for a certain period of time. During that time the company makes and sells the invention and pays the inventor a certain amount of money—a royalty—for each item sold. That arrangement is called "licensing." Both the inventor and the manufacturer make money when a product is sold. That's what Canadians Laura Robinson and Paul Toyne chose to do after they created the board game Balderdash.

When she was growing up in London, Ontario, Canada, Laura Robinson loved playing games with her family. "We had a big family. My mom was a triplet," said Laura. "I have lots of cousins, aunts, and uncles and we'd all play."

One game they loved to play was called Dictionary. They'd find a word that no one knew, make up definitions, and have others guess which was the correct one. "It's fun because it requires imagination. It's the only game I know that guarantees a laugh," said Laura.

Some years later when Laura, her friend Paul Toyne, and other friends were on a ski vacation, Laura suggested they play Dictionary.

It was such fun that Laura and Paul decided to make the game into a product.

First, Laura and Paul spent months at the library of the University of Toronto looking through dictionaries to find "outrageous words," as Laura put it. Once they had the words, they went to companies to find out exactly what it would cost to make the game boards, the boxes, the cards—all the elements of the game. At that time they were thinking of manufacturing the game themselves. They hired an artist to design the board, cards, and box. The result was a model or prototype of the game Balderdash. Anyone could open up the box and play the game.

"It's really important to make as good a prototype as possible," said Laura. It became important to her and Paul when they decided to license the game rather than to manufacture it themselves. Laura thought more people would buy the game if it was produced by a game company. Besides, Laura and Paul had other careers. At the time Laura, an actress, was appearing in commercials and television shows. Paul was an advertising copywriter.

"When we took it to distribution companies, it looked just like a game they could play," said Laura. And that's what people from the companies did: they played the game in the office and at home with their families. That their model of Balderdash looked like a real game worked in Laura and Paul's favor. They made a licensing arrangement with Canada Games, who produced the game with the artwork provided by Laura and Paul. In return Laura and Paul received a royalty payment for each game that was sold.

"When we made our licensing agreement we made it a part of the deal that we'd renegotiate after three years," said Laura. "By that time the game was number one so we were able to get a higher royalty payment."

To protect their product Laura and Paul secured a trademark on the name Balderdash in Canada, the United Kingdom, Australia, the

United States, and Europe. Now the game is sold in all those places. In Sweden the game is translated into Swedish and is called Rapelkalja. More than five million copies of Balderdash have been sold worldwide.

"Five generations of my family played the game at Christmas," said Laura. "I love the idea of bringing families together and of selling laughter." Laura, now married and the mother of two children, is working with her husband, Mark Ettlinger, on producing Balderdash as a television game show.

LICENSING IS A path taken by many inventors who do not want to start their own manufacturing businesses. Young inventors are usually too busy with school to become manufacturers. That's why young inventors often choose to license their products.

Wendy Johnecheck was a fifth-grader at St. Francis Xavier Elementary School in Petoskey, Michigan, in 1984 when a playground equipment company made a licensing agreement with her for the use of her invention Quadro-Jump, an unusual type of jump rope.

It all started with a school assignment. When her teacher, Sister Mary Anne Spanjers, asked the class to do a report on an inventor, Wendy had another idea. She wanted to create an invention instead. As she started thinking, she knew one thing. She loved to jump rope, but it bothered her that it took three friends to play jump rope: two to turn the rope, one to jump. Lots of times Wendy played with just one friend. So she thought and thought. How could she solve that problem?

Wendy lived on a farm. There were lots of pieces of equipment around. She looked at the handle for a shovel and got an idea. She could use the handle to hold one end of the rope. She and her mother,

Wendy Jonecheck's Quadro-Jump. Courtesy of Quality Industries.

Carol Johnecheck, went to the hardware store. Wendy was looking for a swivel device. If she put it on the handle, she could tie a rope to it and the device would swivel or turn. But she couldn't find a device. So she found two different parts to make her own swivel device. When she returned to the farm, her grandfather showed her how to use the electric drill to make a hole in the handle to insert the device. Then she needed a long rope. Her grandfather gave her pieces of used bailer twine that she tied together. Then her two brothers and two sisters helped her braid the pieces until she made a ten-foot piece of rope. Then she braided the rope onto the swivel device and turned the rope while her brothers and sisters jumped. Bingo. Her invention worked.

Wendy thought some more. At school a lot of kids liked to jump rope at the same time. So she attached four swivel devices to the handle. And four ropes. If the handle was stuck in the ground, four could turn a rope and others could jump. So she finished her invention, wound the ropes around the handle, and took it to school. It was an instant hit. Within days a hole for the shovel handle was installed in the playground, and every recess kids would retrieve the jump rope from the office, stick it in the hole, and jump rope. Wendy called it Quadro-Jump.

Sister Mary Anne thought it was a good idea. So when the fifth-graders started their lesson on writing business letters, she thought that the class could benefit by writing to playground equipment companies about Quadro-Jump. Wendy and her mother did some research and discovered several companies in the Midwest. The students wrote letters asking them if they would be interested in manufacturing the jump rope. Many of the companies were not interested. Then Quality Industries of Hillsdale, Michigan, sent a letter expressing interest. They contracted with Wendy and her mother to manufacture Quadro-Jump. Since then, the mid-1980s, Quality Industries has been selling her jump rope all over the United States. They pay Wendy a royalty for the use of her invention. Wendy continued her schooling and has since graduated from Ohio's Wittenberg University. She concentrated on Asian Studies and went to live and teach in Japan.

Manufacturing, selling, or licensing their products are paths taken by inventors. Each inventor makes a choice just like Bette Graham, Rose Totino, Hazelle Rollins, Laura Robinson, and Wendy Johnecheck did. An invention is property. It's an inventor's choice about what to do with the property.

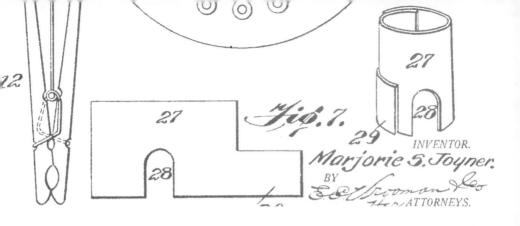

7 *Women Sell Their Inventions*

"I had no idea that people would want that same kind of parenting. We had just come from a culture where everyone carried their kids that way."
—Ann Moore, inventor, Snugli

As the drummer walked up and down the main street in Sokode, Togo, West Africa, the mothers listened. The drum beat out the message that the meeting with the nurse would be outside the hospital later in the afternoon.

Ann Moore, the nurse, met the mothers and their babies when they arrived. As they sat down on chairs set up under a tree, Ann explained what foods would help the babies grow stronger and healthier. As she talked, Ann noticed how peaceful the babies were. The mothers carried the babies on their backs, tied on with a piece of fabric. "The babies seemed so content," Ann thought. When she went home later she told her thoughts to her husband, Mike, who, like Ann, was a Peace Corps volunteer in the small African country in the 1960s. As they worked with the Togolese people, Ann and Mike began to feel that the custom of carrying a child close during the first

Ann Moore at a nutrition clinic in Africa in 1960. Courtesy of Ann Moore.

months of childhood helped the children to have emotional well-being.

After they returned to the United States in 1962, Ann gave birth to their first child, Mande. Because Ann wanted to carry Mande on her back the way the Togolese did, she tried tying her on with fabric. "In Africa they just take that long piece of fabric and swaddle the babies on their back. I could never make it work. She always slid down my back," said Ann. So she sewed together a type of baby carrier with straps like a backpack. She cut holes for Mande's legs. It worked, sort of. Then she turned for help to her mother, Lucy Aukerman, who had made clothes for Ann growing up. "Mom and I worked together on the design and on sewing," said Ann. They proceeded to improve the design and create a baby carrier that is used by millions of mothers and fathers today. Ann called it Snugli because of the way it felt.

While the Snugli is now sold worldwide, then it was only on Ann's back. Ann carried Mande in the Snugli as she did her daily activities. Because Ann and Mike didn't have a car then, they rode their bikes around Denver, Colorado, where they lived. "I had a lot of exposure," she said, "so a lot of people would see the Snugli and say, 'Wow, that looks terrific.'"

After enough other parents asked for a carrier of their own, Ann and her mother decided, "Why not?" "After we started a business, Mother did all the sewing with friends," said Ann. She gained a patent and then made a few changes to the original design. A slight modification made it possible to wear the carrier on the chest or back. A few tucks held baby's head in place. Over the period of a few years, they sold hundreds of baby carriers. Mike, a Yale graduate, helped them manage the business while he worked for a government program called the War on Poverty. The family referred to the business as "Ann's hobby."

Then, in 1968 an article on Snugli appeared in *The Whole Earth Catalogue,* a magazine that reported on alternative, natural ways of living. Snugli received a high rating. Ann's orders went from fifteen to twenty-five a month and continued to rise. Because it was becoming more than a hobby, Mike decided to become more involved in running the business. He and Ann decided to try to increase sales by visiting stores around the United States to sell Snuglis. Buyers for many of the larger stores did not

Ann Moore with her daughter, Mandela, in 1965. Courtesy of Ann Moore.

place orders because they thought Snugli was an item for only a small group of people. But small stores placed orders. They catered to that group of 1960s parents interested in natural ways of caring for their children. Then in 1975 when *Consumer Reports* gave the Snugli a top rating, large stores began ordering as well. "In the 1970s we built a state-of-the-art factory," said Ann. "We made Snugli less expensive by having everything so organized." Customers could also still buy the original handmade version.

By 1985, when Snuglis were sold all over the country, Ann and Mike were running a large company and found that they wanted to make a change. "It wasn't fun anymore," said Ann. "It's always a problem making the cash flow work when you get really big. It was so stressful and we always said that when it lost its joy it would be time to move on." So they sold the company to Gerry Baby Products, a Huffy Company, which continues to manufacture Snugli. After Gerry Baby Products bought the company, they made their own modifications to the design. "Even though I was all prepared knowing it was the right thing, when we signed the papers I started crying on the way home," said Ann. "It was a sense of real loss, it was such a part of us for a long time."

Today Ann is glad. She didn't retire. Her background as a nurse prompted her to invent Air Lift, a backpack for oxygen carriers. Ann and Mike's new company, centered in Evergreen, Colorado, has since added shoulder bags to its product line, which caters to people who need a constant source of oxygen. They can use Air Lift packs and bags to carry small tanks of oxygen so that they can have more active lives. Without the carriers, they are housebound or have to tow the tank on a cart. Ann has also designed a line of nursing bags with the local hospice, and Air Lift is now selling the bags nationally to hospices and home health agencies. "I love what I'm doing now," said Ann. "Our little company is growing but it's still a lot of fun."

Ann Moore didn't set out to create a company with Snugli. "It was a happening," said Ann, who was surprised that she and her mother created an item that was popular with a generation of parents. "It was right at the time when breastfeeding was coming in so it was a natural with people who wanted to go along with breastfeeding and natural childbirth, then to carry the baby close. It all made sense."

Many years earlier, another woman, Sarah Breedlove McWilliams Walker, later known as Madam Walker, started a very different business by selling her products door-to-door in the streets of the African American community.

Sarah was born in Louisiana in 1867. Her parents were former slaves. Her family lived in a windowless, one-room shack on the Mississippi River and slept on the dirt floor. They worked in the

Madam Walker at the wheel. Courtesy of the Indiana Historical Society.

cotton fields during the day. But before Sarah was seven years old, her parents died. She moved in with a married sister, and by age fourteen she was married herself. At age eighteen she gave birth to a daughter, Leila. Two years later her husband was dead.

So that she would have more opportunity, Sarah moved to St. Louis to live near her brother and other relatives. She worked as a cook and washerwoman. To make herself attractive, she did what other African American women did—she used a wrap-and-twist method to straighten her hair. Unfortunately for her, the method made her hair fall out. She experimented with combinations of shampoo and pomade to create a hair treatment to help her with her problem. When she applied it to her scalp, her hair began growing back.

When her friends expressed an interest in buying her hair treatment, Sarah decided to start a business. While she continued working in homes, she began going door-to-door in the African American community and offering not only to sell her hair treatment products, but also to dress the ladies' hair with them in the ladies' homes. She took the unusual step—"The Walker Way"—of applying her hair products with a hot comb, one that was heated on a stove. The comb had teeth that were wide enough for the hair of African Americans.

As Sarah's business was starting, her brother died. With only $1.50 in her pocket, Sarah moved with her daughter, Leila, to Denver. It was there that she met and married C. J. Walker, a newspaperman, and became Madam Walker. He taught her about advertising and the mail-order business. Soon she was successfully promoting her hair-care product. She had labels printed with her picture on them that she pasted on every bottle. They also included the name of her product: Madam C. J. Walker's Hair Grower.

As a way to increase her business, Sarah decided to train others to sell her product. These Walker Agents, as she called them, wore white blouses with long black skirts and carried black satchels to hold the hair-care products. By 1910 she had trained five thousand

Walker Agents. By 1919 the number was twenty-five thousand. They worked on commission and earned generous incomes.

As sales increased, Madam Walker moved to Pittsburgh, Pennsylvania, where she set up a beauty school, Leila College, named after her daughter. She also established a chain of beauty parlors in the United States, the Caribbean, and South America and became the first African American female millionaire in the United States.

And she was flamboyant. She built a mansion for herself on the Hudson River at Irvington, New York, then bought a large convertible and drove around New York City with the top down. The Madam C. J. Walker Manufacturing Company was the most successful company in America owned by an African American woman. She was the president and sole owner.

Madam Walker felt a responsibility to others. She donated to the NAACP, Tuskegee University, and other organizations. And she prompted her agents to be generous as well. She organized them into Walker Clubs and gave cash prizes to the clubs that did the largest amount of community and philanthropic work.

Madam Walker was an entrepreneur. She started a small business and turned it into a large one, just as Ann Moore did. Ann found her customers among the parents of her own generation. Madam Walker found her market in the African American community. Monta Lea Kramer, another entrepreneur, and a quilter from Tennessee, found a market for Q-Snap, her patented quilt frame, by approaching other quilters.

Monta Lea and her husband, an attorney, moved from Illinois to Tennessee to begin their retirement in the 1980s. Once there, Monta Lea decided to learn to quilt. After she joined a group of quilters called "The Jolly Dozen," she had a problem with the quilt frames. They were too bulky or pinched the edge of the fabric.

Then Monta Lea decided to create her own frame. She went out to the workshop, got out a band saw, and sawed up pieces of plastic pipe. To put them together in a square shape for a frame, she attached them to each other with elbow pieces. Then she draped her quilting material over it. But how was she going to make the fabric fit tightly over the square? Then she got the idea to saw other pieces of pipe in half, lengthwise, and snap those half-pieces over the sides of the square. That made the fabric fit tightly. The snapping sound gave her the idea for the name: Q-Snap. Her fellow quilters realized she had created an effective, lightweight frame and wanted ones for themselves. "They weren't doing me a favor," says Monta Lea. "They knew it was good." Q-Snap is now sold worldwide.

Instead of just selling to her neighbors, Monta Lea decided to make one hundred Q-Snaps and to try selling them at the annual American Quilters Society Show in nearby Paducah, Kentucky. "As I drove there with all of the quilt frames loaded in my car, I thought, 'Who am I kidding? No one is going to buy these,'" said Monta Lea.

But that's not what happened. Within two hours she was sold out. She left the show with orders for 350 more Q-Snaps. "It was a real shockeroo," said Monta Lea.

After she returned home, she began making the parts for frames to fill her orders. As she was sitting on her patio surrounded by pieces of plastic pipe, her husband walked out. "I looked at him and I thought, 'I don't think this is the way he was planning to spend his retirement,'" said Monta Lea. So she opened a factory to manufacture her quilt frames. She has since sold more than one million Q-Snaps to quilters and to quilt shops in the United States, Europe, and Asia.

Each inventor takes a slightly different approach in selling her product. Dot Young Kirby sold her Dot Young Sewing Guide through sewing and gift catalogs. She was in her sixties in 1969 when she gained a patent for a sewing guide to top stitch the rounded necklines of jackets, blouses, and collars. Dot had been sewing since she was eight, when she made clothes for her sister's dolls. "Most guides are only helpful with straight edges," said Dot. "I thought the American home sewer deserved something better." Apparently the home sewer agreed. Dot formed Dot Young Enterprises in Clermont, Florida, and sold hundreds of thousands of her guides during the 1970s and 1980s. She ran her business until 1993, when she was eighty-five. She then moved to New Jersey where at age eighty-nine she leads an active life.

While Dot Young Kirby chose to feature her guides in catalogs, Judy Ryder ended up creating a catalog to sell her product. In the mid-1980s, Judy, a mother from Woodland Hills, California, invented Little Shirt Anchors, a device for keeping her baby's shirt down. After she gained a utility patent for a "releasable securing device for an infant's shirt" she began marketing it by placing an ad in a diaper service publication.

When she looked closely at the other ads, she realized they were for other products relating to babies. When she contacted the people who placed the other ads, she discovered they also were "mother-inventors." Judy organized them and created a catalog of mother-invented products. Judy then approached radio and television stations about featuring stories on mother inventors. Both the catalog and the media coverage helped Judy and the other mother-inventors sell their products.

The Internet is the latest selling tool. When computer graphic artist Tana Brinnand wanted to let others know of her invention, she turned to it. Tana, a computer graphic artist, faced a problem shared by many others in her profession who spend so many hours using a keyboard—her wrists hurt. That's what prompted her to design, create, and patent MouseMitt—part glove, part wrist cushion.

Because not many other computer artists lived near her in the small mountain community of Scotts Valley, California, south of San

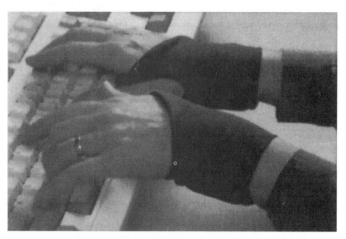

Tana Brinnand's MouseMitts. Courtesy of MouseMitts, Intl.

Francisco, Tana started promoting MouseMitt by sending out press releases to computer magazines and creating a home page on the World Wide Web. Her promotion paid off. After several magazines printed stories, Tana began getting orders. Internet browsers placed orders on her home page. The Internet is a modern tool Tana is using to promote her MouseMitts.

Inventors like Ann Moore, Madam Walker, Monta Lea Kramer, Dot Young Kirby, Judy Ryder, and Tana Brinnand are called independent inventors. After creating their products, they also created businesses to sell their products. While most independent inventors are interested in sales, one independent inventor had another goal.

Leslie Dolman was an engineer who volunteered at West Park Hospital in Toronto, Ontario, Canada. She worked with disabled adults who wanted to get jobs. One of the men she worked with couldn't speak or write. So Leslie made a device that would allow him to work an IBM computer. That was in 1985. "A device did exist with the Apple 2E," said Leslie, "but it was for kids. Nothing existed for adults." Then she designed similar devices to fit the needs of the other disabled adults at the hospital. She called her device PC A.I.D.

and had the name trademarked. "I wanted to use engineering in a way to help people."

As she created more devices, Leslie decided to form a nonprofit corporation, DADA (Designing Aids for Disabled Adults), and interested other engineers, computer programmers, and health care professionals in participating. Salaries of everyone were low, and all profits were poured back into the business. Because each disabled adult had different difficulties working a computer, each device was modified to meet the individual's needs. Some needed a special keyboard, others used a straw to input data, others used Morse code. "Sometimes it was frustrating because for everything you did, it just revealed other things that were needed, more and more ways the device needed to be upgraded," said Leslie. Devices were created for people who spoke German, Spanish, and French.

Leslie didn't apply for a patent. "Our strategy was to sell at such a low price. We didn't think there would be any competition and we didn't want to spend the money getting a patent."

After six years, Leslie wanted to dissolve the corporation. So she designed a sophisticated version of her device and sold it, and the business, to TASH, Inc. (Technical Aids and Services to the Handicapped), of Canada. TASH distributed the devices around the world. Leslie now works at the University of Toronto assisting small businesses that are doing technical projects. She helps them to get their programs funded by the federal government.

Independent inventors are only one type of inventor. Many other women inventors do research and invent as employees of companies that produce drugs to fight disease, make toys for kids, and create materials that will be used in making fabrics for clothing. Some work in laboratories creating food or cleaning products or at aerospace firms creating systems or materials that are used in spacecraft. Although these professionals are the inventors and patent holders, they exchange their employment for the rights to the patents they

Nov. 27, 1928.

M. S. JOYNER

1,693,515

PERMANENT WAVING MACHINE

Filed May 16, 1928

3 Sheets-Sheet 1

Patent drawing for Marjorie Joyner's Permanent Wave Machine.

gain. They assign the rights to the patent to the company that paid for their research and provided the research facilities. When inventors assign the rights to the patent to the company, that means the company, not the inventor, can sell the product. In that situation, inventing is part of a profession.

Marjorie Joyner worked as one of Madam Walker's Walker Agents and became an inventing employee. After she worked for some time as a hairdresser in one of the beauty parlors, Marjorie became frustrated that the method of waving the hair using the hot comb and Madam Walker's products applied with the hot comb lasted for such a short time. So she invented the permanent wave machine, which she patented in 1928 when she was thirty-two. It was used in the beauty parlors. She claimed in her patent that her machine "will wave the hair of both white and colored people."

The permanent wave machine was something to see. It was dome shaped like the modern hair dryers in a beauty salon. On this one, however, curling irons hung by wires from the inside of the dome. How did Marjorie use it? When she started to do someone's hair, she divided the hair, wrapped it in small pieces of flannel, then wound the hair onto the curling irons. She arranged the curling irons so they were away from the scalp, placed a protector over the head, and turned on the electricity. The process set the wave.

Because she created her machine as an employee of Madam Walker's company, Marjorie did not profit directly from the use of her machine. She did, however, become national supervisor of the Madam C. J. Walker Manufacturing Company's chain of nationwide beauty schools and worked for the company for many years. She told author Anne L. Macdonald in *Feminine Ingenuity: Women and Invention in America*, "I never got a penny from it, but that's OK. . . . I don't have a whole loaf of bread but I have a thick slice. I have my health; I have a beautiful home of my own." Marjorie Joyner lived to be ninety-eight years old. The *Washington Post* hailed her as the "Grand Dame of Black Beauty Culture." In the years preceding her death, she was president of the charities of the *Chicago Daily Defender*, the African American paper of that city. When she was ninety-three, Marjorie Joyner was honored by the Forty-fourth National Convention of the National Council of Negro Women in its "Salute to Black Women Who Make It Happen." She died when she was ninety-four.

For other women who pursue careers in the sciences, inventions are only part of their professional achievement. Their inventions allow them to pursue their work and to achieve their goals.

That describes the professional life of Dr. Ellen Ochoa. In 1990 Dr. Ellen Ochoa became the first Hispanic woman astronaut selected by NASA. She is also a coinventor on three patents. During the 1980s, when Ellen was at Stanford University working toward a master of science degree and a doctorate in electrical engineering and doing research at Sandia National Laboratories, she was interested in optical systems used for processing information. One of her patents is for an optical inspection system. "NASA looks for people who have accomplished a lot in their careers, people who have published papers and gotten patents," said Ellen. "I didn't consider a career in science when I was in junior high, but it is a good field because you can be judged concretely on the work you do."

As an astronaut, Ellen has flown in space for twenty days, a total of 484 hours. She used a robot arm to deploy and capture the Spartan satellite. Now she works at NASA's mission control center talking to crews of astronauts up in space.

Scientist, biologist, and inventor Dr. Ruth Patrick of Philadelphia, Pennsylvania, has also invented as part of her career. When Ruth was growing up in Kansas, her father, Frank Patrick, a lawyer and banker with an interest in science, took her and her sister on Sunday walks to the river. With a tin can attached to a bamboo pole, they would gather algae from the rocks, troop home, and examine it under a microscope. "He'd show me things under the microscope. They were beautiful in the refracted light. I was enchanted with the

Ruth Patrick. Courtesy of the Academy of Sciences.

shapes, colors, and movement," said Ruth. She and her sister were looking at diatoms, the microorganisms that are at the bottom of the food chain. "By the time I was twelve, he was asking me to name the different diatoms I'd see under the microscope."

Those early experiences in the 1910s led Ruth to continue studying diatoms as an adult. She completed a Ph.D. program at the University of Virginia at Charlottesville, then used her knowledge of diatoms to study different bodies of water. That's what led her to devise and patent the Diatometer. It is a floating Plexiglas holder device for microscope slides. It is placed in lakes or rivers or the sea for several weeks, during which time the microorganisms of the aquatic community attach to the slides. When it is removed from the water, a scientist can look at the slides and determine if and how much the water is polluted. They make their judgment based on the number and type of diatoms because diatoms do not thrive in polluted water. "I designed the Diatometer to face upstream so that the current was equal on all the slides," said Ruth. "The light exposure had to be right as well. I wanted something that would provide a uniform collection of diatoms so I could compare those from upstream with those from downstream. A steel bar weights it." Ruth's contribution to ecology, by way of her Diatometer, is to alert scientists to the importance of looking at the entire aquatic community to determine water quality.

In her work as one of the nation's leading biologists, Ruth has studied many American rivers and led an expedition of scientists to Peru and Brazil in 1955 to study the quality of water of the Amazon River. During World War II, when a U-boat was captured off the east coast of the United States, Ruth was called in to analyze the diatoms scraped off the side of the ship. Because diatoms from different areas have a different appearance, she was able to determine where the ship was from.

During Ruth's career, she has been an advisor to Presidents Johnson, Carter, Reagan, and Bush and received from President Clinton the National Medal of Science Award in 1996. She celebrated her eighty-ninth birthday that same year. She works several days a week at the Academy of Sciences in Philadelphia where in 1947 she founded the Department of Limnology—the scientific study of freshwater rivers and lakes.

Selling an invention can have many definitions. Many independent women inventors have created successful businesses to market their products which have enriched the economy of the world. Other women inventors have worked for companies doing research that has led to the creation of products that cure diseases, make home life easier, increase safety, provide fun, and help with the exploration of the earth and of space. The contributions of women inventors are an intricate part of world history and economy.

8 An Inventor's Resource Guide

Books about Inventors and Inventing

Brown, Kenneth A. *Inventors at Work*. Redmond, WA: Tempus Books of Microsoft Press, 1988.

Caney, Steven. *Steven Caney's Invention Book*. New York: Workman Publishing Co. Inc., 1985.

Coleman, Bob, and Deborah Neville. *The Great American Idea Book*. New York: W. W. Norton & Company, 1993.

Flack, Jerry D. *Inventing, Inventions, and Inventors: A Teaching Resource Book*. Englewood, CO: Teacher Ideas Press, 1989. (Available from Teacher Ideas Press, Department T963, P.O. Box 6633, Englewood, CO, 80155-6633.)

Gardner, Robert. *Experimenting with Inventions*. New York: Franklin Watts, 1990.

Gerardy, Nancy. *Invention Log*. (Available from the Center for Gifted Education, 3211 1-70 Drive, S.W., Columbia, MO, 65203.)

Griffin, L., and K. McCann. *The Book of Women: 300 Notable Women History Passed By*. Holbrook, MA: Bob Adams, 1992.

Grissom, Fred, and David Pressman. *The Inventor's Notebook.* Berkeley, CA: Nolo Press, 1989.

Haskins, Jim. *Outward Dreams: Black Inventors and Their Inventions.* New York: Walker & Co., 1991.

James, Portia P. *The Real McCoy: African American Invention and Innovation,* 1619-1930. Washington, D.C.: Smithsonian Press, 1989.

Jeffrey, Laura S. *American Inventors of the 20th Century.* Springfield, NJ: Enslow Publishers, Inc., 1996.

Karnes, Frances A., and Suzanne M. Bean. *Girls and Young Women Inventing.* Minneapolis, MN: Free Spirit Publishing, Inc., 1995.

Macaulay, David. *The Way Things Work.* Boston: Houghton Mifflin, 1988.

Macdonald, Anne L. *Feminine Ingenuity: Women and Invention in America.* New York: Ballantine Books, 1992.

Moussa, Farag. *Women Inventors Honored by the World Intellectual Property Organization.* Geneva, Switzerland: Coopi, 1991. (For more information contact: International Federation of Inventors' Associations, 3 Rue Bellot CH1206, Geneva, Switzerland. Phone: 41 22 789 3074 or Fax: 41 22 789 3076.)

Murphy, Jim. *Weird and Wacky Inventions.* New York: Crown Publishers, Inc., 1978.

Panabaker, Janet. *Inventing Women: Profiles of Women Inventors.* Ontario, Canada: Women Inventors Project, 1991. (For more information contact: Women Inventors Project, 107 Holm Crescent, Thornhill, Ontario L3T 5J4. Phone: 905-731-0328 or Fax: 905-731-9691.)

Showell, Ellen H., and Fred M. B. Amram. *From Indian Corn to Outer Space: Women Invent in America.* Petersborough, NH: Cobblestone Publishing, Inc., 1995.

Taylor, Barbara. *Be an Inventor.* New York: Harcourt Brace Jovanovich, 1987.

Thompson, Charles. *What a Great Idea!* New York: Harper
Perennial, 1992.
Tucker, Tom. *Brainstorm: The Stories of Twenty American Kid Inventors*.
New York: Farrar, Straus, and Giroux, 1995.
Vare, Ethlie Ann, and Greg Ptacek. *Mothers of Invention*. New York:
William Morrow and Company, Inc., 1988.
Vare, Ethlie Ann, and Greg Ptacek. *Women Inventors and Their
Discoveries*. Minneapolis, MN: The Oliver Press, 1993.
Weiss, Harvey. *How to Be an Inventor*. New York: Thomas Y.
Crowell, 1980.

Books about Patenting and Marketing Your Invention

Drew, Bonnie, and Noel Drew. *Fast Cash for Kids*. Franklin Lake,
NJ: Career Press, 1995.
Jones, Stacy V. *Inventions Necessity Is Not the Mother of—Patents
Ridiculous and Sublime*. New York: Quadrangle/The New York
Times Book Company, 1973.
Levy, Richard C. *The Inventor's Desktop Companion: A Guide to
Successfully Marketing and Protecting Your Ideas*. New York: Visible
Ink Press, 1991.
Park, Robert. *The Inventor's Handbook: How to Develop, Protect, and
Market Your Invention. Second Edition*. Cincinnati, OH: Betterway
Books, Inc., 1990.
Pressman, David. *Patent It Yourself. Fifth Edition*. Berkeley, CA: Nolo
Press, 1996.
Richardson, Robert O. *The Weird and Wondrous World of Patents*. New
York: Sterling Publishing Co., Inc., 1990.
Ryder, Judy. *Turning Your Great Idea into a Great Success*. Princeton,
NJ: Peterson's/Pacesetter Books, 1995.

Internet Sites

Key words to help you browse the Internet include:

inventions

young inventors

women inventors

lemelson center (Lemelson National Program in Invention and Innovation at Hampshire College has information about individual inventors and unusual patents.)

www.uspto.gov/ and **ftp.uspto.gov.** This site contains general information about patents and trademarks.

U.S. Patent and Trademark Office
General Information Services Division
Crystal Plaza 3, Room 2Co2
Washington, D.C. 20231
Phone: 1-800-786-9199
Fax: 703-305-7786

Write for one of these free booklets:

Basic Facts about Patents (GIS-5010P-PP). This free booklet provides a brief overview of the patent application process.

Basic Facts about Registering a Trademark (GIS-5020T-PP). This free booklet provides information about registering a trademark.

web.mit.edu/invent This site has invention related links and resources and features an inventor every week.

www.girltech.com This site has information specifically about women and girl inventors and the National Inventors Hall of Fame.

www.idye.com This site offers publications for young entrepreneurs ranging in age from early teens to early thirties. Young entrepreneurs from more than forty countries are members.

The Young Entrepreneurs Network and International Directory
of Young Entrepreneurs
376 Boylston Street, Suite 304
Boston, MA 02116
Phone: 617-867-4690
Fax: 617-267-3057

www.kidsites3000.com KIDBIZ is an interactive workshop for kids
ages twelve through sixteen interested in inventing or creating. Click
away to find out about patents, trademarks, the history of inventions,
and business. Kids are invited to submit pictures of themselves and
their inventions. Experts in a variety of fields are available online to
consult with kids about their ideas and about starting their own businesses for less than fifty dollars.

Places to Visit

Inventure Place, the National Inventors Hall of Fame
221 South Broadway Street
Akron, OH 44308
Phone: 330-762-6565 or 1-800-968-IDEA
Fax: 330-762-6313
Internet: http://**www.invent.org/**

Inventure Place houses the National Inventors Hall of Fame.
Information about the inventors and their inventions are on display.
Interactive exhibits give visitors a hands-on look at lasers, video ani-
mation, magnetism, and much more. Workshops on Saturday morn-
ings allow participants of any age to figure out how to launch an egg
into space and other challenges. Also located at Inventure Place is
the National Gallery for America's Young Inventors. Why have a
gallery for inventions by kids? Why not? In 1996 six young inventors, grades kindergarten through twelve, were inducted into the
gallery.

The first inductees included Kara Levine, of New York, who developed Karink, a newspaper printing ink that reduces air pollution; seniors Elizabeth Nathan and Gabriella Pollack, both of New York, who invented a nonreusable syringe that would help decrease the spread of AIDS; Alexia Abernathy, a ninth-grader from Iowa, who created the Oops! Proof No-Spill Feeding Bowl for children who are learning to feed themselves; Christopher Cho, of New York, who invented an Automated Page-Replacing Contrivance for musicians that allows them to turn pages of music with a foot pedal rather than with their hands; Johnny K. Bodylski, a third-grader from California, who invented The Rain Watchdog that automatically turns off a water sprinkler when it begins raining and turns it on when the water evaporates; and Peter C. Haugen, an eleventh-grader from North Dakota, who invented the Interfaceable Refreshable Braille Display Prototype Using Shape Memory Wires that allows the blind to use computers, calculators, and control systems.

To qualify for nomination the students must: 1)have been a finalist in a national competition; 2) have a device that is being manufactured or 3) have an invention that is in the process of being patented or is patented.

Judges: Outstanding students from around the country who are on the Student Board of Directors review, nominate, and select the inductees. An adult Board of Advisors oversees them. The adult Board includes members of the National Science Teachers Association, Duracell employees, scientists, teachers, and business people.

Awards: Inclusion in the National Gallery for America's Young Inventors

Administrators: The Partnership for America's Future, a nonprofit educational organization comprised of business people and public-school teachers

Sponsors: Businesses, granting agencies, and individuals

For information contact:

The National Gallery for America's Young Inventors
c/o The Partnership for America's Future
80 West Bowery Street, Suite 305
Akron, OH 44308-1148
Phone: 330-376-8300
Fax: 330-376-0566
E-mail: pafinc@aol.com

Invention Camps

Camp Invention-Open to kids in grades one through five
221 South Broadway Street
Akron, OH 44308
Phone: 330-762-6565 or 1-800-968-IDEA
Fax: 330-762-6313

Why not go to a camp for inventors? Kids in grades one through five take part in a one-week summer day camp. The variety of activities include a take-apart activity in which kids take apart broken appliances, clocks, radios, telephones, etc., and use the parts for a new invention, and one in which they create working models of amusement park rides.

Camp Invention began as an educational activity of Inventure Place in Akron, Ohio. More than fifty camps take place each summer in the counties around Akron. Camps are also being held in other cities including Boston, San Diego, Columbus, Cincinnati, Baltimore, Long Island, Pittsburgh, Tampa/St. Petersburg, New Hampshire, Chicago, St. Louis, and other cities. Call the number listed to find the city nearest you. Cost for a one-week camp is approximately $100-$150.

Camp Ingenuity-Open to kids in grades six through eight
c/o Inventure Place
221 South Broadway Street
Akron, OH 44308
Phone: 330-762-6565 or 1-800-968-IDEA
Fax: 330-762-6313

Why not go to a camp where you can be ingenious, clever, and smart? Activities at this one-week residential camp for boys and girls in grades six through eight concentrate on different real-world problems to solve: building a free-standing structure, designing a communication system using lasers and sound, or inventing a new fast food or sport. Campers also participate in the YMCA's leadership training course which includes high-ropes and low-ropes challenges plus swimming and boating. The camp is administered by Inventure Place and takes place at a center on the YMCA grounds near Akron, Ohio. Camp takes place in August. Cost is approximately $375.

Toledo Area Science and Invention Camp
c/o Burroughs Elementary School
2404 South Avenue
Toledo, OH 43609
Contact: Sally Duncan, Director
Phone: 419-382-2232

This program is sponsored by the Toledo Public Schools and the Toledo Association for the Promotion of Inventive Thinking. It is open only to students in grades one through five in Ohio schools. At this one-week summer camp students invent, try out kitchen physics, take a close look at bugs, and use chemistry skills with play dough and glue.

Invention Programs and Contests

Invention programs sponsored by schools, companies, and organizations take place all over the United States. Some are national programs. Others are local, county, or state programs that feed into national programs.

NATIONAL COMPETITIONS AND PROGRAMS IN THE UNITED STATES

Young Inventors and Creators Program

Open to: Students in all fifty states in grades seven through twelve. As individuals with the signature of the school principal or through school programs.

Deadline: June

Description: Students submit inventions they are working on and they are judged by a system that is similar to but separate from the official patent application process. There are school, regional, and state competitions that lead to the national competition. However, any individual student, with the signature of his or her school principal, is eligible to enter an invention. Students, through their schools or individually, submit their inventions to coordinators who oversee regional judging. (Students may also work in teams of two or three.)

Inventions can be submitted in the following categories:

Health Invention

Invention for Business/Office Use

Household/Food Invention

Agricultural Invention

Invention for New Technology

Leisure Time/Entertainment Invention

Environmental Invention

Transportation/Travel Invention

As in patent applications, students have to include the title of the invention, a written explanation of how they got the idea, how the invention works, what it is used for, and drawings, photographs, or videotapes that best illustrate the invention. And as would happen at the U.S. Patent and Trademark Office, entries are judged according to originality or novelty, usefulness, and on the drawings and the written description.

Judges: Educators

Sponsors: National Inventive Thinking Association, the U.S. Patent and Trademark Office, the U.S. Copyright Office, and Hampshire College in cooperation with Patent and Trademark Depository Libraries and Centers for the Book

Awards: Regional or state participants receive certificates of participation; winners receive certificates of achievement. National winners will be recognized at the National Creative and Inventive Thinking Skills Conference held each year in November. More than ten thousand students have participated.

For rules and entry forms contact:

National Inventive Thinking Association
P.O. Box 836202
Richardson, TX 75083
or
Office of Public Affairs
U.S. Patent and Trademark Office
Washington, D.C. 20231
Phone: 703-305-8341

The Annual Duracell/NSTA Scholarship Competition

Open to: Students in grades nine through twelve who work with a teacher/sponsor

Deadline: Early January

Description: The challenge is to create and build devices powered by Duracell batteries. Student inventors submit a wiring diagram, an essay, and an entry form to the National Science Teachers Association (NSTA), which administers the program. Finalists are asked to present working models. Students retain all rights to their devices. The entries are judged on creativity, practicality, the energy efficiency of the battery-powered device, and the clarity of their essay.

First Step: As a way to help participants prepare for the contest, Duracell initiated First Step, an optional program that allows students to submit concepts for their battery-powered devices to professionals who then make evaluations and give suggestions. Students can then build devices with the suggestions. First Step is independent of the formal competition.

Judges: Scientists and science educators selected by the NSTA

Awards: $100,000 in prizes. Every student who completes an entry receives a certificate of recognition and an entry gift. One hundred students receive awards and personalized certificates. Teachers/sponsors of the top one hundred finalists receive gifts. The first-place winner receives a $20,000 U.S. Series EE savings bond. Five second-place winners receive $1,000 bonds. Twenty-five fourth-place winners receive $500 bonds. Up to fifty-nine finalists receive $200 bonds. Teachers/sponsors of the first- and second-place winners receive personal computers.

The top six winners present their inventions and receive their awards at the annual NSTA convention. Along with their parents and sponsoring teachers, they are guests of Duracell at these award festivities held in St. Louis each March.

Judges: Members of NSTA and science educators

Sponsors: Duracell USA and administered by the NSTA

For rules and entry forms contact:

The Annual Duracell/NSTA Scholarship Competition
c/o National Science Teachers Association
1840 Wilson Boulevard
Arlington, VA 22201
Phone: 703-243-7100
E-mail: ecrossley@nsta.org

Partnership for America's Future

Open to: Any student in grades kindergarten through twelve

Deadline: A contest is held every month

Description: Partnership for America's Future, a nonprofit educational organization comprised of business people and public school teachers, was created to encourage exchange between students and the business community. Businesses contribute genuine problems they need solved, such as how to create a shield to block radio waves or how to prevent birds from congregating in certain spots. Students who come up with ideas for products that solve these and other problems posed by the partnership may win a monthly prize. If one of the businesses makes a product based on a student's idea, the student can collect royalties.

Judges: Business people and experienced high school teachers

Awards: Prizes of $50 to monthly winners plus royalties if products are created

Sponsors: Partnership for America's Future, a nonprofit program developed and run by full-time public school teachers

Send your ideas to:

Partnership for America's Future
80 West Bowery Street, Suite 305
Akron, OH 44308
Phone: 330-376-8300
Fax: 330-376-0566
E-mail: pafinc@aol.com

The Silver Burdett & Ginn Invention Convention

Open to: Students in grades one through six at schools using Silver Burdett & Ginn science textbooks

Deadline: February

Description: Silver Burdett & Ginn is a textbook publishing company that sponsors the annual Invention Convention for students in kindergarten through sixth grade, in schools that use their science books. The Invention Convention can be a classroom-, school-, or district-wide science event. Participants are encouraged to identify a need to solve a problem by following the same steps and procedures as an inventor would follow in patenting an invention.

Local Invention Conventions held at schools select only one primary student (first through third grade) and one intermediate student (fourth through sixth grade) to represent their school in the Annual International Invention Convention.

Judges: For local contests, judges are selected by local organizers and usually include science teachers from both high schools and universities as well as outstanding science students. Judges for the international Invention Convention include distinguished inventors, scientists, and teachers.

Sponsor: Silver Burdett & Ginn

Awards: Local winners receive Patent Certificates. Prizes vary for winners of the national and international Invention Convention, but two winners receive a personal computer, and the top winner and his or her parents receive an all-expenses paid trip to the ceremony held at the national meeting of National Science Teachers Association.

For rules and entry forms contact:

The Silver Burdett & Ginn Invention Convention
c/o Silver Burdett & Ginn
Attention: Karen Schenk
299 Jefferson Road
Parsippany, NJ 07054

STATEWIDE INVENTION PROGRAMS AND COMPETITIONS IN THE UNITED STATES

Programs exist at thousands of individual schools and classrooms across the country. Some states host statewide invention programs, and they are listed here. If a state is not listed, inquire at the local school district or enter one of the national programs listed previously.

Connecticut

Connecticut Invention Convention

Open to: Students in Connecticut

Deadline: Varies

Description: Connecticut students are challenged to create original inventions. Ten percent of the inventors from each school are selected to participate in the statewide Connecticut Invention Convention.

Judges: Inventors, engineers, corporate representatives, and educators

Sponsors: Local school districts

For rules and entry forms contact:

Connecticut Invention Convention

Attention: Michelle Munson, Chair

15 Humphrey Street

Concord, NH 03301

Phone: 603-271-2717

Florida

Invent Broward

Open to: Students in kindergarten through fifth grade in Broward County

Deadline: School Deadlines vary in preparation for Invention Broward Showcase that is held in April or May

Description: A non-competitive program. Broward County Library is a Patent and Trademark Depository. To educate students about inventions and patents, they send representatives out to visit schools, share a traveling display, and encourage students to brainstorm about inventions. Students are also invited to visit the Patent and Trademark Depository within the library to learn the skills of doing a patent search. At their schools, students work out their ideas and make models that are showcased in the library at the end of the school year. More than six hundred models are presented each year at a reception honoring the young inventors.

Awards: Certificates and badges for all participants in the showcase

Sponsors: Broward County Library and Broward County School System

For rules and entry forms contact:
Invent Broward
Broward County Library
Attention: Marie Moisdon
100 S. Andrews Avenue
Ft. Lauderdale, FL 33301
Phone: 954-357-7376

Iowa

Invent, Iowa!

Open to: Iowa students in grades kindergarten through eight

Deadline: Varies

Description: Students are asked to create inventions that benefit mankind, the earth, the disabled, and seniors by solving a problem encountered in everyday life. Students participate by taking part in local invention conventions run by Iowa's Area Education Agencies. When it started in 1987, three hundred students participated. By the mid-1990s more than thirty thousand students in public, private, and in-home schools participated. Regional and district competitions are run by Iowa's Area Education Agencies. Regional winners compete in the annual State Invention Convention held in Des Moines, Iowa, each April, and all participants receive an honorary patent.

Judges: Educators and business people

Awards: Certificates

Sponsors: Businesses, foundations, and organizations in Iowa

For rules and entry forms contact:

Invent, Iowa!
Attention: Dr. Nicholas Colangelo, Program Director
c/o The Connie Belin Center at the University of Iowa
210 Lindquist Center
Iowa City, IA 52242-1529
Phone: 319-335-6148 or 1-800-336-6463

Minnesota

Minnesota Student Inventors' Congress

Open to: Minnesota students in grades kindergarten through twelve
Description: Students first take part in invention activities at the local level. Regional competitions are then hosted by the state's nine Educational Cooperative Service Units. A maximum of twelve inventions from each region are invited to be displayed in a noncompetitive environment in conjunction with the annual Minnesota Inventors Congress in Redwood Falls in June.
Judges: Adult inventors and educators
Awards: Selection for participation in Minnesota Inventors Congress
Sponsors: Minnesota Educational Cooperative Service Units (ECSU)
For rules and entry forms contact:
Minnesota Student Inventors Congress
Attention: Kate Martens, State Coordinator
South Central ECSU
1610 Commerce Drive
North Mankato, MN 56003
Phone: 507-389-5766 or the coordinators at your regional ECSU

New Hampshire

New Hampshire Young Inventors' Program

Open to: New Hampshire students in grades kindergarten through eight

Deadline: April

Description: Classrooms and schools host invention programs and select an invention to represent each grade in a school at the annual Young Inventors' Celebration for New Hampshire.

The criteria for judging is originality, usefulness, marketability, illustration or model presentation, written description, and research (content only for grades kindergarten through three).

New Hampshire challenges its young inventors to create in two special categories. The first is a medical invention—one that solves a health-related problem. This category is judged by a representative of the New Hampshire Medical Association. Winners receive U.S. Savings Bonds and an invitation to the New Hampshire Medical Association Annual Meeting.

The second category is a Rube Goldberg—one based on the creations of cartoonist Reuben Goldberg, who poked fun at modern technology by creating devices with moving parts that complicate simple tasks. What does that mean? A sixth-grader created a Rube Goldberg Automatic Balloon Popper which popped a balloon with a dart. How? Drop a golf ball in a funnel that leads to a hose, watch for the ball to come out of the hose and then roll through a mailbox, down a circular track, and onto a mousetrap to set off a rubber band trigger that propels the dart to pop the balloon.

Judges: Engineers, business owners, mayors, past Young Inventors, teachers, and retirees

Awards: Winners are chosen in the following categories for each grade level: most outstanding, environmental, special needs, fun and leisure time, practical and useful, and original and unique. There is also an Inventors' Choice Award selected by the participating inventors. Each inventor receives a certificate of participation.

Sponsors: Academy of Applied Science and private donations

For rules and entry forms contact:

New Hampshire Young Inventors' Program
Academy of Applied Science
98 Washington Street
Concord, NH 03301
Phone: 603-228-4530

New Jersey

Student Inventions Through Education (SITE)

Open to: Students in New Jersey schools in grades kindergarten through twelve

Deadline: Varies with school

Description: Thirteen thousand kids a year participate in this twenty-year-old program in which students individually or in teams develop an invention during the school year. Students keep a log as they progress. For local and regional competitions students give oral presentations to judges and demonstrate a working prototype.

Judges: Educators and members of the business community

Awards: Medallions and plaques for the regional events

Sponsors: New Jersey Department of Education

For rules and entry forms contact:
Student Inventions Through Education (SITE)
Educational Information Resource Center
606 Delsea Drive
Sewell, NJ 08080
Phone: 609-582-7000

New York

Western New York Invention Convention Program

Open to: Students in western New York

Description: Students participate in invention programs in their individual schools. One invention from each school is chosen to be displayed for three days in May at Erie Community College. A lunch is staged for winning students and their parents. Plaques are given to participating schools.

Judges: Business people

Awards: Certificates, savings bonds

Sponsors: Businesses, local colleges, and community members

For rules and entry forms contact:

 Western New York Invention Convention Program

 c/o Buffalo Public Schools Early Childhood Center

 428 City Hall

 Buffalo, NY 14202

 Phone: 716-851-3626 or 716-851-3627

Ohio

Project Outreach

Open to: Anyone in Ohio, in grades seven through twelve, in teams of three to ten members working with an advisor under the sponsorship of a community organization such as a school, church, or club

Description: An educational problem-solving program for teens that focuses on developing creative solutions to community problems. Teams of teenagers respond to six annual challenges on topics including illiteracy, voter education, toys for teaching, and teen action.

Judges: Community leaders of Dayton and surrounding areas

Sponsors: Local universities, service clubs, and businesses

For rules and entry forms contact:

 Inventors Council of Dayton

 Attention: Ron Versic

 140 East Monument Avenue

 Dayton, OH 45402

 Phone: 513-224-8513

 or

Project Outreach
9258 Clyo Road
Dayton, OH 45458
Phone: 513-885-2301
E-mail: rwatkins@infinet.com

Oklahoma

Oklahoma Student Inventors Exposition, Inc.

Open to: Oklahoma students in grades kindergarten through twelve

Deadline: Varies for local programs but the statewide program culminates in February with a display of inventions at the state capitol

Description: Since this invention program is an exposition, the emphasis is on the process and creation of inventions rather than on competition. Guidelines are patterned after the patent application guidelines of the U.S. Patent and Trademark Office. Each student is asked to create a poster that includes a drawing and description of their invention and to submit a log book that shows their progress. Those who participate in local school invention programs are eligible to be selected to have their invention displayed at the state capitol each February. The Oklahoma Student Inventors Exposition is always held when the state legislature is in session so that students also have an opportunity to meet their legislators.

Judges: Science students and members of the Department of Commerce

Awards: Trophies, ribbons, certificates, and cash prizes for both teachers and students

Sponsors: Oklahoma Invention Development Society

For rules and entry forms contact:

Oklahoma Student Inventors Exposition, Inc.
Attention: Betty Wright
3804 Larkwood Drive
Del City, OK 73115
Phone: 405-670-3131 or 405-231-2000
Fax: 405-670-3872

Oregon

Future Makers: Inventor/Mentor Program

Open to: Middle school students in Oregon and Washington

Description: Want to help out a business? That's the point of the Future Makers Program. Students in sixth through ninth grades learn the techniques of inventing. Then they are teamed up with business people who escort them to their places of business and ask the students to come up with solutions to real problems in the workplace. Student teams work on solutions. One manufacturing plant had a problem with efficient delivery to their loading dock. Students designed a color-coded package-sorting system for the loading area. Students visited a fast-food chain then worked on inventing a box to keep french fries hot. Other students visited the Nike shoe factory and invented the "Air Ballet" dance shoe for Nike. The program culminates with an Invention Convention where students present ideas in a science fair type of event. More than fifteen thousand students in Oregon and Washington have participated.

Sponsors: A program of the Saturday Academy, the pre-college education center of Oregon Graduate Institute of Science & Technology. Developed with funds from the National Science Foundation.

For rules and entry forms contact:
Future Makers Program, Saturday Academy
c/o Oregon Graduate Institute
P.O. Box 91000
Portland, OR 97291-1000
Phone: 503-690-1190

Tualatin Invention Program

Open to: Elementary school students in Oregon

Deadline: Ongoing

Description: First-grade teacher Evelyn Andrews of Tualatin Elementary School is an invention curriculum enthusiast. She offers materials for kindergarten through sixth about invention to all Oregon schools. Students think of ideas and create inventions. Adults act as advisors.

Sponsors: Individual schools

For rules and entry forms contact:

Tualatin Invention Program

c/o Tualatin Elementary School

Attention: Evelyn Andrews

19945 S.W. Boones Ferry Road

Tualatin, OR 97062

Phone: 503-684-2359

Index